Sedgewood®Press

Published by Sedgewood Press

For Sedgewood ® Press
Director Elizabeth P. Rice
Associate Editor Leslie Gilbert
Production Manager Bill Rose

Published for Sedgewood ® Press by
Marshall Cavendish Books Limited
58 Old Compton Street
London W1V 5PA

For Marshall Cavendish
House Editor Dorothea Hall
Editor Sally Harding
Designer Sheila Volpe

First Printing 1986

© Marshall Cavendish Limited 1986
Distributed by Macmillan Publishing Company,
a division of Macmillan, Inc.

ISBN 0–02–609140–2
Library of Congress Catalog Card
Number 85–51795

Printed in the United States of America

INTRODUCTION

The pleasure and satisfaction in hand knitting for babies and children combined with economy makes it one of the most popular crafts today.

There is a wonderful range of yarns available in exciting colors and textures. There are pure wool, cotton and synthetic varieties, and several mixed fiber yarns to choose from. With the addition of man-made fibers the practicability of many yarns has recently been greatly improved, so that hand knits, (especially for babies and children) can be machine-washed with complete confidence – this also includes some pure wools.

With this superb selection of 45 patterns bolstered by the comprehensive know-how section, you'll find knitting for babies and children most rewarding – creating garments you'll be proud to have made.

CONTENTS

Chapter 1
BABY KNITS

Knitting for a new baby is always a delightful and rewarding experience. Many small items can be made relatively quickly, at little cost – using left-over yarns for edgings and embroidered details. In the following pages you'll find a superb collection of pretty pastel-colored blankets, coats, bonnets, mitts and dresses to suit baby boys and girls from birth to nine months.

The stitch patterns range from very simple stockinette stitch, as in the Sailboat Pants on page 17, and the mittens on page 25, to the raised leaf medallions of the baby blanket and the delicate lacy stitch of the Matinée Set (see pages 9 and 19). The traditional Cumbrian Crib Quilt on page 12 offers a more unusual stitch technique and a wonderful opportunity to create your own rainbow-colored effect for a new layette.

Leaf Blanket

Keep baby warm and snug in this soft patchwork blanket decorated with embossed leaves, eyelets and delicate embroidery.

Size
Width 20½"
Length 29½"

Materials
- ☐ 10oz of a knitting worsted weight yarn
- ☐ Small amounts of 2 contrasting colors
- ☐ Set of five size 6 double-pointed knitting needles
- ☐ Tapestry needle

Gauge
1 square measures 9½" by 9½" using size 6 needles.

To save time, take time to check gauge.

Note The blanket is made of square medallions which are knitted separately and then sewn together. Each medallion is worked in rounds from the center outward. The edging is worked in a long strip which is joined after completion to the outer edge of the patches.

Square medallion (make 6)
Using four needles, cast on 8 sts – 2 sts on each needle (see Helping Hand).
Use the fifth needle to work in rounds as foll:
1st round K tbl to end.
2nd round (K into the front and back of the stitch) 8 times. 16 sts.
3rd round (P1, K1, P2) 4 times.
4th round (P1, yo, K1, yo, P2) 4 times.
5th round (P1, K3, P2) 4 times.
6th round (P1, K1, yo, K1, yo, K1, P2) 4 times.
7th round (Yo, P1, K5, P1, yo, P1) 4 times.
8th round (P2, K2, yo, K1, yo, K2, P3) 4 times.
9th round (Yo, P2, K7, P2, yo, P1) 4 times.
10th round (P3, K3, yo, K1, yo, K3, P4) 4 times.
11th round (Yo, P3, K9, P3, yo, P1) 4 times.
12th round (P4, K4, yo, K1, yo, K4, P5) 4 times.
13th round (Yo, P4, K11, P4, yo, P1) 4 times.
14th round (P5, K5, yo, K1, yo, K5, P6) 4 times.
15th round (Yo, P5, K13, P5, yo, P1) 4 times.
16th round (P6, K6, yo, K1, yo, K6, P7) 4 times.
17th round (Yo, P6, K15, P6, yo, P1) 4 times.
18th round (P7, K7, yo, K1, yo, K7, P8) 4 times.
19th round (Yo, P7, K17, P7, yo, P1) 4 times.
20th round (P8, yarn to back of work – called ybk-, sl 1-K1-psso, K13, K2 tog, P9) 4 times.
21st round (Yo, P8, K15, P8, yo, P1) 4 times.
22nd round (P9, ybk, sl 1-K1-psso, K11, K2 tog, P10) 4 times.
23rd round (Yo, P9, K13, P9, yo, P1) 4 times.
24th round (P10, ybk, sl 1-K1-psso, K9, K2 tog, P11) 4 times.
25th round (Yo, P10, K11, P10, yo, P1) 4 times.
26th round (P11, ybk, sl 1-K1-psso, K7, K2 tog, P12) 4 times.
27th round (Yo, P11, K9, P11, yo, P1) 4 times.
28th round (P12, ybk, sl 1-K1-psso, K5, K2 tog, P13) 4 times.
29th round (Yo, P12, K7, P12, yo, P1) 4 times.
30th round (P13, ybk, sl 1-K1-psso, K3, K2 tog, P14) 4 times.
31st round (Yo, P13, K5, P13, yo, P1) 4 times.
32nd round (P14, ybk, sl 1-K1-psso, K1, K2 tog, P15) 4 times.
33rd round (Yo, P14, K3, P14, yo, P1) 4 times.
34th round (P15, ybk, sl 1-K2 tog-psso, P16) 4 times
35th round (P15, K1, P16) 4 times.
36th round *Yo, K1, (yo, sl 1-K1-psso) 15 times, yo, P1, rep from * 3 times.
37th round K to end.
38th round *Yo, K1, (yo, sl 1-K1-psso) 16 times, yo, P1, rep from * 3 times.
39th round K to end.
40th round *Yo, K1, (yo, sl 1-K1-psso) 17 times, yo, P1, rep from * 3 times.
41st round P to end.
42nd round (Yo, K to last st on needle, yo, P1) 4 times.
43rd round P to end.
Bind off loosely.
Make five more squares.

Leaf edging
Using two needles, cast on 8 sts.
Work in rows as foll:
1st row K5, yo, K1, yo, K2.
2nd row P6, K twice into next st, K3.
3rd row K4, P1, K2, yo, K1, yo, K3.
4th row P8, K twice into next st, K4.
5th row K4, P2, K3, yo, K1, yo, K4.
6th row P10, K twice into next st, K5.
7th row K4, P3, K4, yo, K1, yo, K5.
8th row P12, K twice into next st, K6.
9th row K4, P4, ybk, sl 1-K1-psso, K7, K2 tog, K1.
10th row P10, K twice into next st, K7.

11th row K4, P5, ybk, sl 1-K1-psso, K5, K2 tog, K1.

12th row P8, K twice into next st, K2, P1, K5.

13th row K4, P1, K1, P4, ybk, sl 1-K1-psso, K3, K2 tog, K1.

14th row P6, K twice into next st, K3, P1, K5.

15th row K4, P1, K1, P5, ybk, sl 1-K1-psso, K1, K2 tog, K1.

16th row P4, K twice into next st, K4, P1, K5.

17th row K4, P1, K1, P6, ybk, sl 1-K2 tog-psso, K1.

18th row P2 tog, bind off 5 sts knitwise using the P2 tog to bind off the first stitch, P3, K4. 8 sts. The first-18th rows form pat and are rep throughout. Cont in pat until edging measures approx 102½″ ending with an 18th row. Do not break off yarn. Slip sts onto a st holder.

To finish

Join squares in three rows of two squares to make a rectangle. Pin edging around outer edge of rectangle, gathering it slightly at the corners. Adjust length of edging if required, always ending with an 18th row. Bind off loosely and sew edging in place.

Using two contrasting colors, embroider the central leaf ribs on the squares and edging with chain stitch (see page 163) and the center of each square with lazy daisy stitch flowers (see page 163). Pastel colors are a pretty combination.

HELPING HAND

Working medallions in the round

Working with five needles may seem a handful if you have never attempted it before. The first round is the most difficult as the needles can slip out easily, so work tightly.

1 *Using the cable method (see page 138), cast on the required number of stitches onto one needle, using an even tension.*

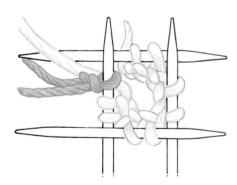

2 *Taking care not to twist the stitches distribute them evenly among four of the set of five needles. Place a marker loop in a contrasting color at the left-hand end to mark the beginning of the round. This will help to make counting subsequent rounds easier.*

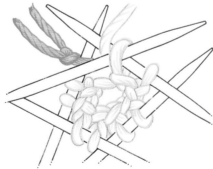

3 *Use the fifth needle as the working needle. Knit every stitch in the first round through the back of the loops to twist them, then continue as instructed in the pattern watching the tension between needles. Slip the marker loop at the beginning of each round.*

VARIATIONS

The blanket can easily be made larger by working more squares and piecing them together. The edging will also have to be made longer to fit the outside border. To vary the size of the squares themselves use a different yarn. A finer yarn will produce a smaller square and a thicker yarn a larger square. Finally, any square medallion pattern could be used instead of the leaf medallion given here.

Cumbrian Crib Quilt

Brighten up baby's room with a beautiful traditional English Cumbrian crib quilt. Choose delicate pastel shades of a machine washable yarn.

Size
Width 20½"
Length 32¼"

Materials
- ☐ 3½ oz of a fingering weight yarn in main color MC
- ☐ 1¾ oz in each of 5 contrasting colors A, B, C, D, and E
- ☐ One pair of size 1 knitting needles

Gauge
16 sts and 22 rows to 2" over St st using size 1 needles.

To save time, take time to check gauge.

Note The quilt is made of triangular patches which are knitted separately and then sewn together.

Full patch (make 43)

Using MC, cast on 60 sts by the thumb method (see Helping Hand).

1st row (WS) K to end.

2nd row *K2 tog, yo, rep from * to last 2 sts, K2.

3rd row K to end.

4th row With MC, K3, K2 tog, K to last 5 sts, K2 tog, K3.

5th row K3, P to last 3 sts, K3.

6th row As 4th row.

7th row As 5th row.

8th row K3 MC, with A K2 tog, K to last 5 sts, K2 tog, K3 MC.

9th row K3 MC, with A K to last 3 sts, K3 MC.

10th row K3 MC, with A P2 tog, P to last 5 sts, P2 tog, K3 MC.

11th row As 9th row.

12th row As 10th row.

13th row With MC, as 5th row.

14th row With MC, as 4th row.

15th row With MC, as 5th row.

16th row With MC, as 4th row.

17th row K3 MC, with B P to last 3 sts, K3 MC.

18th row K3 MC, with B P2 tog, P to last 5 sts, P2 tog, K3 MC.

19th row K3 MC, with B K to last 3 sts, K3 MC.

20th row As 18th row.

21st row As 19th row.

Rep 4th-21st rows once more, using C instead of A and D instead of B. Then work 4th-12th rows using E instead of A. 14 sts.

Using MC, cont in garter st (K every row), dec one st in center of each row until one st rem.

Fasten off.

Make 42 more full patches in the same way.

Left-hand side border patch

Using MC, cast on 30 sts by the thumb method.

1st-3rd rows Work as for full patch.

4th row K3, K2 tog, K to end of row.

5th row K1, P to last 3 sts, K3.

6th row As 4th row.

7th row As 5th row.

8th row K3 MC, with A K2 tog, K to end of row.

9th row With A, K to last 3 sts, K3 MC.

Worked in bands of pretty pastel colors, the cot quilt patch is a slight variation of the traditional one-color Cumbrian patch.

10th row K3 MC, with A P2 tog, P to last st, K1.
11th row As 9th row.
12th row As 10th row.
Cont in this way, foll color sequence given for full patch, and working garter st border at beg of RS rows only, and dec as before inside this edge only. K the last st on RS rows and the first st on WS rows throughout.
Cont until 3 sts rem.
Next row With A, K2 tog, K1.
Next row K to end.
Next row K2 tog.

Fasten off.
Work 7 more border patches in the same way.

Right-hand side border patch
Work as for left-hand side border patch, reversing garter st border and shaping to the other side. Work 7 more border patches.

To finish
Do not press.
Sew patches tog as shown in photograph, reversing three patches to fit top edge.

HELPING HAND

Thumb method of casting on
This method of casting on will provide the fine, elastic edge necessary for the Cumbrian patches.

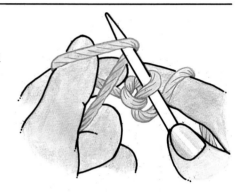

1 *Make a slip loop 25" from the end of the yarn. Place it on the needle. Hold the yarn from the ball in your right hand and wrap the long end around the left thumb. Insert the needle under the loop on the thumb.*

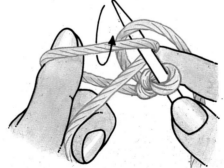

2 *Take the yarn from the ball under and over the point of the needle and bring it through the loop on the thumb to make a new stitch.*

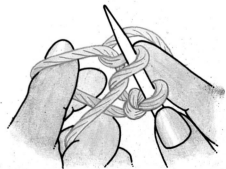

3 *Slip the loop off the thumb. Pull the yarn to tighten the stitch. Wrap the yarn around the thumb as before and repeat these steps for the required stitches. A 25" end is enough for about 60 stitches.*

VARIATIONS
Originating in the English Lake District about two hundred years ago, Cumbrian knitting has a delightfully old-fashioned appeal. Traditionally it is worked in soft, lightweight cotton yarn in either white or cream. These authentic materials produce a delightful play of light and shade over the surface of the fabric, but many other types of yarns are equally suitable. Because Cumbrian knitting is a form of patchwork which uses a number of triangular shapes pieced together, a quilt of any size can be made simply by adding more triangles. Since the exact size of the quilt can be varied in this way there should be no problems about using different yarns. If a thicker yarn is used the size of the patch will, of course, be larger and fewer patches will be needed. Making a Cumbrian quilt is a perfect way to use up leftover yarns!

Wave Lace Smock

The skirt of this smock is knitted in a simple wave lace. Neckline, hem and sleeves are bordered with a subtle stripe in a contrasting color.

Back

Using smaller needles and MC, cast on 135 sts. Work 3 rows in garter st (K every row).
Change to larger needles and work in wave lace pat as foll:
**1st row (RS) K1, *K2, sl 1-K2 tog-psso, K2, yo, rep from * to last st, K1.
2nd row P1, *P6, yo, rep from * to last st, P1.
The first two rows form wave lace pat.

Work 3 more rows in pat. Change to smaller needles.
Next row (WS) K to end.
Join in A and K 2 rows.
Next row With MC, K to end.
Next row With MC, K1, *K6, yo, rep from * to last st, K1. **
Change to larger needles. Rep from ** to **. Change to larger needles and cont in wave lace pat until back measures 7¾" from beg, ending with a 2nd row.***

Size
To fit 18" chest or newborn to 6 month old baby
Length 14¼"

Materials
☐ 3½oz of a fingering weight yarn in main color MC
☐ Small amount in contrasting color A
☐ One pair each of sizes 2 and 3 knitting needles
☐ 4 buttons

Gauge
30 sts and 33 rows to 4" over wave lace pat using size 3 needles.

To save time, take time to check gauge.

Note Back and front of dress are each worked in one piece from hem to neck.

Divide for back opening
Next row Work 65 sts in pat, turn and leave rem 70 sts on a st holder. Cont in pat on these 65 sts for right side of back opening until back measures 10¼″ from beg, ending with a 2nd row.
Change to smaller needles.
Next row (RS) (K2 tog) to last 3 sts, K3 tog. 32 sts.
Work 5 rows in St st, beg with a P row.
Shape armhole
Cont in St st, bind off 3 sts at beg of next row.
Work one row.
Dec one st at armhole edge on next 3 rows.
Work one row.
Dec one st at armhole edge on next row and then on every other row once. 24 sts.
Work even in St st until back measures 4″ from beg of armhole shaping, ending with a P row.
Shape shoulder
Bind off 5 sts at beg of next row and then on every other row twice.
Work one row. Sl rem 9 sts onto a safety pin.
Return to sts on left side of back opening. With RS facing, sl first 5 sts at center back onto a larger safety pin. Rejoin MC, and using larger needles, work in pat to end of row. 65 sts.
Complete to match right side, reversing shaping.

Front
Work as for back to ***.
Work 2¼″ in wave lace pat, ending with a first row. Change to smaller needles.
Next row (WS) P1, (P2 tog) to end. 68 sts.
Work 4 rows in St st, beg with a K row.
Shape armholes
Bind off 3 sts at beg of next 2 rows; dec one st at each end of next 3 rows.
Work one row.
Dec one st at each end of next row and every other row once. 52 sts.
Work even in St st until front

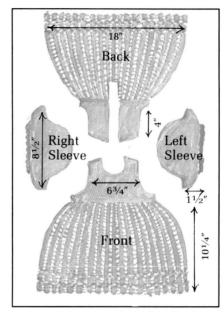

measures 12 rows less than back to shoulder shaping, ending with a P row.
Shape neck
Next row K21, K2 tog, turn and leave rem sts on a st holder.
Complete left side of neck first. Dec one st at neck edge on next 4 rows and then on every other row 3 times. 15 sts. Work one row.
Shape shoulder
Bind off 5 sts at beg of next row and then every other row once.
Work one row.
Bind off rem 5 sts.
Return to sts at right side of neck. With RS facing, sl first 6 sts at center front onto a safety pin. Rejoin yarn.
Next row K2 tog, K to end. 22 sts.
Complete to match left side of neck, reversing shaping.

Sleeves (make 2)
Using smaller needles and A, cast on 32 sts. Work 3 rows in garter st (K every row). Join in MC.
Next row K1, (pick up strand between st just worked and next st and K into back of it, K1) 31 times. 63 sts.
Cont in St st until sleeve measures 1½″ from cast-on edge, beg and ending with P row.

Shape cap
Bind off 3 sts at beg of next 2 rows.
Dec one st at each end of next row and then every other row until 45 sts rem, ending with a P row.
Dec one st at each end of every row until until 33 sts rem.
Bind off 2 sts at beg of next 2 rows.
Next row K1, *K2 tog and bind off st on right-hand needle, rep from * to end. Fasten off.

Button band
Using smaller needles and MC, cast on 5 sts. Cont in garter st (K every row) until band, when slightly stretched, fits up right back opening, beg and ending with a WS row. Leave sts on a safety pin.

Buttonhole band
With RS facing, using smaller needles and MC, K5 from safety pin at center back. Work as for button band, working one buttonhole level with beg of St st yoke and two others at 1½″ intervals.
Work buttonhole rows on RS as foll:
Buttonhole row K1, K2 tog, yo, K to end.

Neckband
Join shoulder seams. Sew on button band.
Using size 2 needles and A, K5 from buttonhole band, K9 from left back neck, pick up and K12 sts down left side of front neck, K6 from center front, pick up and K12 sts up right side of neck, K9 from right back neck, K5 from button band. 58 sts.
Work 4 rows in garter st, making 2nd row a buttonhole row.
Bind off loosely.

To finish
Join side and sleeve seams. Set in sleeves. Sew button border behind buttonhole border on WS at base of opening. Sew on buttons.
Press seams lightly on WS with warm iron.

Sailboat Pants

These baby's pants with a sailboat motif are made in two simple pieces. Make them in a machine washable yarn in the color of your choice.

Back
Using larger needles, cast on 13 sts.
1st row K to end.
2nd row P to end.
Cont in St st, cast on 3 sts at beg of next 12 rows. 49 sts.
Inc one st at each end of every row until there are 75 sts.
Work even in St st until back measures 8¼" from cast-on edge, ending with a P row.
Shape back

Next row K70, turn.
Next row Sl 1, P64, turn.
Next row Sl 1, K59, turn.
Cont in this way, working 5 sts less on every row until the row "sl 1, P14, turn" has been worked.
Next row Sl 1, K to end.
Next row P to end.
** Change to smaller needles and work in rib as foll:
1st row K1, * P1, K1, rep from * to end.

Size
To fit 9 month old baby

Materials
☐ 2oz of a machine washable sport weight yarn in main color MC
☐ Small amounts in each of 3 contrasting colors
☐ One pair each of sizes 3 and 6 knitting needles
☐ 20" of ½"-wide elastic
☐ Tapestry needle

Gauge
22 sts and 28 rows to 4" over St st using size 6 needles.

To save time, take time to check gauge.

Note Each piece is worked from crotch to waist.

17

Sailboat motif

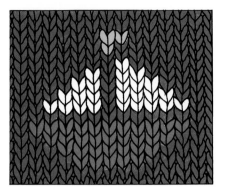

2nd row P1, * K1, P1, rep from * to end.

Rep last 2 rows for ¾", ending with a first row.

Next row K to end to form ridge. Beg with a first row, work in rib for ¾". Bind off loosely in rib.**

Front

Using larger needles, cast on 13 sts.
1st row K to end.
2nd row P to end.
Cont in St st, inc one st at each end of every row until there are 45 sts.
Cast on 3 sts at beg of next 10 rows. 75 sts.
Work even until front measures 8¼" from beg, ending with a P row. Work in rib from ** to ** as on back.

Leg borders

Join crotch seam.
Using smaller needles and with RS facing, pick up and K63 sts around the leg.
Work in K1, P1 rib for 2".
Bind off in rib.

To finish

Join side seams and leg borders.
Fold leg borders in half to WS and sew in place. Fold waistband in half to WS and sew in place, leaving a space to insert the elastic. Join remaining seam.
Using contrasting colors and tapestry needle, embroider motif, foll the colored chart. (See page 50 for duplicate stitch.) Press seams lightly on WS with warm iron.

HELPING HAND

Working a band with elastic

The best method for working bands with elastic for baby garments is to work a double width band in ribbing. The center can be marked by a fold line. The band is then folded in half and stitched in place, leaving an opening. The elastic is then threaded through, the ends joined and the opening closed.

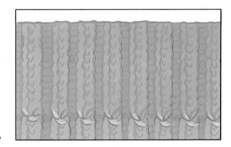

1 Work in K1, P1 rib until half the band is completed, ending with a right side row. Knit the next row. This makes a ridge on the right side. Continue in rib, working one row less than for first half of band. Bind off loosely in rib.

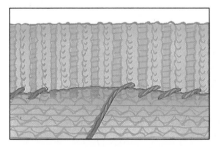

2 When side seams have been joined, fold the band in half onto the wrong side of the work and sew in place, leaving an opening of about 2" for the elastic.

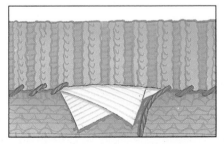

3 Thread the elastic through opening and join both ends to form a circle. Ease the elastic back into the band and join opening.

Matinée Set

Knit this pretty and practical matinée set. It is worked in a delicate lacy stitch and will fit a baby from birth to six months old.

Size
To fit 18″ chest or newborn to 6 month old baby
Length 10½″
Sleeve seam 5″

Materials
☐ 7oz of a fingering weight yarn
☐ One pair of size 3 knitting needles
☐ 6 small buttons
☐ 3 yd of narrow ribbon
☐ Size B crochet hook

Gauge
32 sts and 40 rows to 4″ over St st using size 3 needles.

To save time, take time to check gauge.

Note Work the lacy pattern loosely and avoid pulling the yarn too tightly, so that the "K4 tog" in the pattern is easier to work.

Jacket

Back and fronts
Back and fronts are worked tog to armhole.
Cast on 261 sts very loosely. K 5 rows.
Beg pat as foll:
1st row (RS) Sl 1, K4, * yo, K8, yo, K1, rep from * to last 4 sts, K4.
2nd row Sl 1, K5, * P8, K3, rep from * to last 3 sts, K3.
3rd row Sl 1, K5, * yo, K8, yo, K3, rep from * to last 3 sts, K3.
4th row Sl 1, K6, * P8, K5, rep from * to last 2 sts, K2.
5th row Sl 1, K6,* yo, K8, yo, K5, rep from * to last 2 sts, K2.
6th row Sl 1, K7, * P8, K7, rep from * to last st, K1.
7th row Sl 1, K7, * K4 tog tbl, K4 tog, K7, rep from * to last st, K1.
8th row Sl 1, K to end.
The first-8th rows form pat. Cont in pat until jacket measures 6" from beg, ending with a WS row.
Divide for first armhole
Next row Work 67 sts in pat, pick up strand between st just worked and next st and work into back of it – called M1 –, turn.
Cont in pat on these 68 sts for 2" for right front, ending with 8th row of pat.
Leave these sts on a spare needle. Rejoin yarn to rem sts.
Next row Work 127 sts in pat, turn.
Cont on these sts for 2" for back, ending with same pat row as on right front.

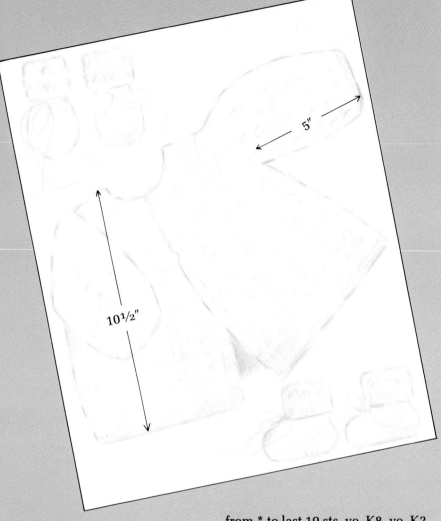

Divide for 2nd armhole
Rejoin yarn to rem sts, M1, work in pat to end.
Cont on these 68 sts for 2" for left front, ending with same pat row as right front.
Leave sts on a spare needle.

Sleeves (make 2)
Cast on 37 sts. K 5 rows.
Next row K1, * M1, K1, rep from * to end. 73 sts.
Beg pat as foll:
1st row (RS) K1, * yo, K8, yo, K1, rep from * to end.
2nd row K2, * P8, K3, rep from * to last 10 sts, P8, K2.
3rd row K2, * yo, K8, yo, K3, rep from * to last 10 sts, yo, K8, yo, K2.
4th row K3, * P8, K5, rep from * to last 11 sts, P8, K3.
5th row K3, * yo, K8, yo, K5, rep from * to last 11 sts, yo, K8, yo, K3.
6th row K4, * P8, K7, rep from * to last 12 sts, P8, K4.
7th row K4, * K4 tog tbl, K4 tog, K7, rep from * to last 12 sts, K4 tog tbl, K4 tog, K4.
8th row K to end.
Rep these 8 rows until sleeve measures 5", ending with same pat row as on back and fronts to division for armholes. Place a marker at each end of this row.
Cont in pat for 2", ending with an 8th pat row.
Leave sts on a spare needle.

Yoke

With RS facing, sl all sts from pieces onto left-hand needle in foll order: left front, sleeve, back, sleeve and right front. 409 sts.
Next row K1, * K2 tog, rep from * to end. 205 sts.
Next row K11, (K2 tog, K16) 10 times, K2 tog, K to end. 194 sts.
K 3 rows.
Next row K11, (K2 tog, K15) 10 times, K2 tog, K to end. 183 sts.
K 3 rows.
Next row K10, (K2 tog, K14) 10 times, K2 tog, K to end. 172 sts.
K 3 rows.
Cont dec on every 4th row as before until 84 sts rem. Bind off.

To finish

Do not press.
Join sleeve seams to markers, stitch remaining sleeve seam into armholes.

Work 6 crochet button loops on right front of yoke.
Sew on buttons to correspond with button loops.

Bonnet

Main piece

Cast on 99 sts very loosely. K 5 rows.
Work in pat as for back and fronts of coat until bonnet measures approx 5″, ending with an 8th pat row.
Shape crown
Next row (K9, K2 tog) 9 times. 90 sts.
Next and every other row K to end.
Next row (K8, K2 tog) 9 times. 81 sts.
Cont dec on every other row as before until the row "(K2 tog) 9 times" has been worked.
Next row (K1, K2 tog) 3 times. 6 sts.

Break off yarn and thread end through rem sts. Pull to gather and fasten off securely.

To finish

Join crown seam. Cut two lengths of ribbon 31½″ long. Sew on ribbons, making loops at each side.

Mittens

Main piece

Cast on 37 sts very loosely.
K 5 rows.
Work in pat as for sleeves of jacket for 16 rows, so ending with a WS row.
Next row Inc in first st, P to last st, inc in last st. 39 sts.

Last row forms a ridge for fold line.
1st row K1, * P1, K1, rep from * to end.
2nd row P1, * K1, P1, rep from * to end.
Rep last 2 rows 9 times more.
Work first row once.
Next row (eyelet row) K1, (yo, K2 tog, K3) 7 times, yo, K2 tog, K1.
** Work 30 rows in garter st (K every row).
Shape top
Next row K5, K2 tog, (K6, K2 tog) 4 times. 34 sts.
Next row K4, K2 tog, (K5, K2 tog) 4 times. 29 sts.
Next row K3, K2 tog, (K4, K2 tog) 4 times. 24 sts.
Cont dec on every row as before until 9 sts rem.
Next row (K1, K2 tog) 3 times. 6 sts.
Break off yarn and thread end through sts. Pull to gather and fasten off securely.

To finish
Join seam. Cut two lengths of ribbon 10″ long.
Thread ribbon through holes at wrist and tie in a bow.

Bootees

Main piece
Work as for mittens to **.
Next row K to end.
Divide for foot
Next row K25, turn.
Next row K11, turn.
Work 20 rows in garter st on these 11 sts.
Break off yarn.
With RS facing, rejoin yarn to inside edge where sts were left and using same needle, pick up and K10 sts along side of instep, K11 instep sts, pick up and K10 sts along other side of instep, K last 14 sts. 59 sts.
Work 10 rows in garter st.
Shape foot
1st row K2, K2 tog, K19, K2 tog, K9, K2 tog tbl, K19, K2 tog tbl, K2.
2nd and every other row K to end.
3rd row K2, K2 tog, K18, K2 tog, K7, K2 tog tbl, K18, K2 tog tbl, K2.
5th row K2, K2 tog, K17, K2 tog, K5, K2 tog tbl, K17, K2 tog tbl, K2.
7th row K2, K2 tog, K16, K2 tog, K3, K2 tog tbl, K16, K2 tog tbl, K2.
8th row K to end.
Bind off loosely.

To finish
Fold bootee in half and join back and foot seam.
Cut ribbon into 20″ lengths and thread ribbon through row of holes.

Coat, Bonnet and Mittens

Worked in a bicolor slipstitch pattern, the coat has smart matching accessories. The snug mittens are worked in stockinette stitch and the bonnet in seed stitch.

Coat
Back
Using size 3 needles and MC, cast on 91 sts. Work in K1, P1 rib as follows.
1st row K1, *P1, K1, rep from * to end.
2nd row P1, *K1, P1, rep from * to end.
Rep last 2 rows for ¾", ending with a 2nd row. Change to size 5 needles and beg pat as foll:

1st row (RS) With A, K2, *sl 1 purlwise, K1, rep from * to last st, K1.
2nd row With A, K2, * yarn to front of work, sl 1 purlwise, yarn to back of work – called sl 1 with yarn in front (wyif), K1, rep from * to last st, K1.
3rd and 4th rows With MC, K to end.

Size
To fit 18" chest or newborn to 6 month old baby
Coat length 14¼"
Sleeve seam 7"

Materials
- ☐ 5 oz of a fingering weight yarn in main color MC
- ☐ 1¾ oz in contrasting color A
- ☐ One pair each of sizes 2, 3 and 5 knitting needles
- ☐ 20" of ¼"-wide ribbon
- ☐ 5 small buttons

Gauge
Coat: 27 sts and 51 rows to 4" over pat using size 5 needles.
Bonnet: 24 sts and 50 rows to 4" over seed st using size 3 needles.
Mittens: 30 sts and 33 rows to 4" over St st using size 3 needles.

To save time, take time to check gauge.

5th row With A, K1, *sl 1 purlwise with yarn in back of work (wyib), K1, rep from * to end.

6th row With A, K1, * sl 1 wyif, K1, rep from * to end.

7th and 8th rows As 3rd and 4th rows.

The first-8th rows form pat and are rep throughout.

Work 14 rows in pat.

Keeping pat correct, dec one st at each end of next row and then every 12th row until 75 sts rem.

Work even until back measures approx 10¼″ from cast-on edge, ending with a 2nd or a 6th pat row.

Shape armholes

Keeping pat correct, bind off 3 sts at beg of next 2 rows. Dec one st at each end of next 5 rows, then at each end of every other row twice. 55 sts.

Work even until back measures 4″ from beg of armhole shaping, ending with a WS row.

Shape shoulders

Bind off 4 sts at beg of next 8 rows. Leave rem 23 sts on a spare needle.

Left front

Using size 3 needles and MC, cast on 52 sts.

1st row *K1, P1, rep from * to last 2 sts, K2.

2nd row P2, *K1, P1, rep from * to end.

Rep last 2 rows for ¾″, ending with a first row.

Next row Rib 7 and leave these sts on a safety pin, rib to end. 45 sts.

Change to size 5 needles and work 22 rows in pat as for back.

Dec one st at beg of next row and then every 12th row until 37 sts rem.

Work even until front measures same as back to armhole shaping, ending with a WS row.

Shape armhole

Bind off 3 sts at beg of next row. Work one row in pat. Dec one st at armhole edge on next 5 rows. Work one row in pat. Dec one st at armhole edge on next row and then on every other row once. 27 sts.

Work even until front measures 12 rows less than back to shoulder shaping, ending with a WS row.

Shape neck

Next row Work 21 sts in pat, K2 tog, turn and leave rem 4 sts on a safety pin.

Work one row in pat. Dec one st at neck edge on next row and then on every other row until 17 sts rem. Work one row in pat.

Shape shoulder

Next row Bind off 4 sts, work in pat to last 2 sts, K2 tog.

Work one row in pat. Bind off 4 sts at beg of next row and then on every other row once. Work one row in pat.

Bind off rem 4 sts.

Right front

Using size 3 needles and MC, cast on 52 sts.

1st row (RS) K2, *P1, K1, rep from * to end.

2nd row *P1, K1, rep from * to last 2 sts, P2.

Rep the last 2 rows for ¾″, ending with a first row.

Next row Rib 45 sts, turn and leave rem 7 sts on a safety pin.

Change to size 5 needles.

Complete to match left front, reversing all shaping.

Sleeves (make 2)

Using size 3 needles and MC, cast on 41 sts. Work in K1, P1 rib as for back for ¾″, ending with a 2nd row.

Next row Rib 3, pick up strand between st just worked and next st and work into back of it – called M1 –, (rib 7, M1) 5 times, rib 3. 47 sts.

Change to size 5 needles and work in pat as for back. Inc one st and work into pat at each end of 5th row and then every 12th row until there are 57 sts.

Work even until sleeve measures approx 7″, ending with a 2nd or a 6th pat row.

Shape cap

Bind off 3 sts at beg of next 2 rows.

Dec one st at each end of next row and then every other row until 25 sts rem.

Bind off 2 sts at beg of next 2 rows and 3 sts at beg of next 2 rows.

Bind off rem 15 sts.

Neckband

Join shoulder seams.

With RS facing and using size 3 needles and MC, K4 sts from right front center neck, pick up and K13 sts up right side of neck, K23 sts of back neck inc 2 sts evenly, pick up and K13 sts down left side of neck, then K4 from left front center neck. 59 sts.

Beg with a 2nd row, work in K1, P1 rib as for back for ¾″. Bind off loosely in rib.

Button band

With RS facing and using size 3 needles and MC, join in yarn to 7 sts at left front, inc into first st, rib 6. 8 sts.

Work in rib as foll:

1st row (WS) P2, (K1, P1) 3 times.

2nd row (K1, P1) 3 times, K2.

Rep these 2 rows until band is long enough, when slightly stretched, to fit up left front to top of neckband. Bind off in rib.

Sew band to front edge. Mark position of 4 buttons, the first level with armhole shaping, the 4th in center of neckband, with rem two spaced evenly between.

Buttonhole band

With WS facing and using size 3 needles and MC, join in yarn to 7 sts on right front, inc in first st, rib 6. 8 sts.

Work in rib as foll:

1st row (RS) K2, (P1, K1) 3 times.

2nd row (P1, K1) 3 times, P2.

Rep these 2 rows until band, when slightly stretched, fits up right front on top of neckband, making buttonholes opposite markers as foll:

1st buttonhole row (RS) Rib 3, bind off 2 sts, rib to end.

2nd buttonhole row Rib to end,

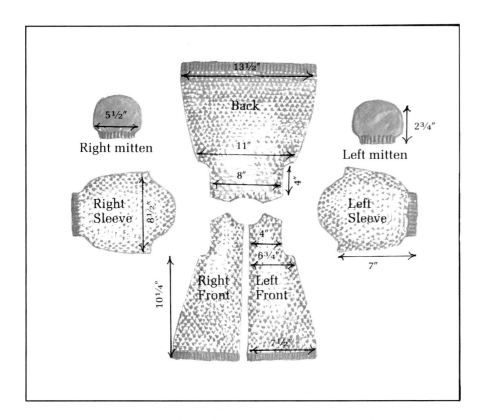

casting on 2 sts over those bound off in previous row.

To finish
Sew on buttonhole band. Join side and sleeve seams. Set in sleeves. Sew on buttons.
Press seams lightly on WS with warm iron.

Bonnet

To make
Using size 3 needles and MC, cast on 81 sts.
1st row K1, *P1, K1, rep from * to end.
This row forms seed st pat. Cont in pat until piece measures 4¼" from beg.
Shape back
Keeping pat correct, bind off 27 sts at beg of next 2 rows. 27 sts.
Dec one st at each end of 5th row and then every 8th row until 15 sts rem.
Work until piece measures 4¼" from beg of back shaping.

Keeping pat correct, bind off.

Lower border and strap
Join back seams.
With RS facing and using size 3 needles and MC, pick up and K20 sts along left side, 13 sts along back, and 20 sts along right side. 53 sts.
Next row Cast on 30 sts, K1, (P1, K1) 41 times.
Cont in seed st, work 2 rows.
1st buttonhole row Work to last 5 sts, bind off 2 sts, work to end.
2nd buttonhole row Work to end, casting on 2 sts over those bound off in previous row.
Work 2 rows. Keeping pat correct, bind off.

To finish
Sew on button. Do not press.

Mittens

To make
Using size 2 needles and MC, cast on 34 sts; work in K1, P1 rib for ¾". Make ribbon slots as foll:

Next row K1, *yo, K2 tog, rep from * to last st, P1.
Next row Rib to end.
Change to size 3 needles.
Next row K5, pick up strand between st just worked and next st and K into back of it – called M1 –, (K8, M1) 3 times, K5. 38 sts.
Cont in St st until piece measures 2¾", beg and ending with a P row.
Shape cap
1st row (K1, K2 tog, K13, sl 1-K1-psso, K1) twice.
2nd and every other row P to end.
3rd row (K1, K2 tog, K11, sl 1-K1-psso, K1) twice.
5th row (K1, K2 tog, K9, sl 1-K1-psso, K1) twice.
7th row (K1, K2 tog, K7, sl 1-K1-psso, K1) twice.
9th row (K1, K2 tog, K5, sl 1-K1-psso, K1) twice.
Bind off rem 18 sts.

To finish
Do not press. Join seam.
Cut piece of ribbon in half and thread through ribbon slots.

Chapter 2
PULLOVERS, VESTS & JACKETS

One of the most attractive aspects of hand knitting garments for small children is that you can add that extra special touch that means so much. Whether you prefer simple or more ambitous designs, here there are plenty of exciting and colorful ideas for ages one to ten (chest sizes 22″ – 32″) to suit all levels of skill.

Stitch techniques are varied and include simple color stripes and contrast edgings, picture motifs like the duplicate stitched ice-cream motif on page 31, and fun fabric appliqué, as on the Train Vest and Kangaroo Sweater (see pages 45 and 76). There are also some stunning color stitch patterns with intricately textured surfaces such as the Slipstitch Top on page 36 and the Loop Stitch Sweater on page 72, and a dazzling variety of charted color designs (see pages 62 and 87) which you could easily adapt to garments of your choice.

Bicolor Zipper Top

The zippers on this sweater make it very versatile. It can be worn with one blue and one yellow sleeve, or with the sleeves zipped off, it can be worn as a spring top.

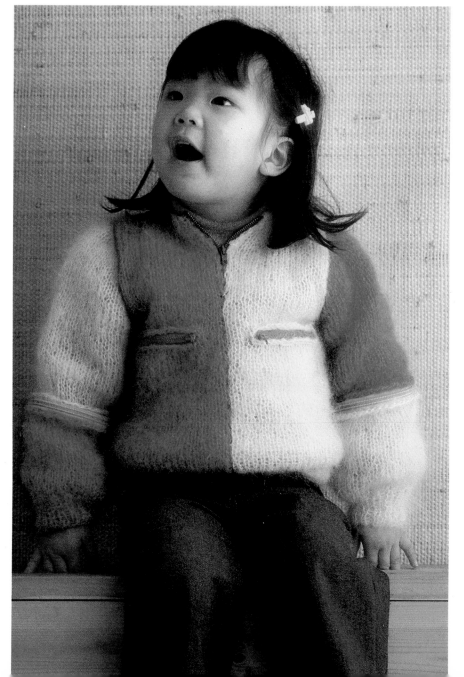

Sizes
To fit 24[26]" chest
Length 16½[18]"
Sleeve seam 10½[12]"

Note Instructions for larger size are in brackets [ ]; where there is only one set of figures it applies to both sizes.

Materials
☐ 4oz of a lightweight mohair in each of 2 colors A (blue) and B (yellow)
☐ One pair each of sizes 3 and 7 knitting needles
☐ Two 4" zippers in red
☐ One 4" zipper in green
☐ Two 12" open-ended zippers in blue
☐ Sewing thread in 2 colors matching A and B for zippers

Gauge
15 sts and 24 rows to 4" over St st using size 7 needles.

To save time, take time to check gauge.

Bicolor Zipper Top

Back right panel

** Using smaller needles and A, cast on 25[27] sts.
1st row K1, * P1, K1, rep from * to end.
2nd row P1, * K1, P1, rep from * to end.
Rep these 2 rows until panel measures 2[2½]″ from beg.
Change to larger needles. Work in St st, beg with a K row.**
Cont in St st until panel measures 11½[12¼]″ from beg, ending with a WS row.

Shape armhole

Bind off 3 sts at beg of next row.
Dec one st at armhole edge on every other row twice. 20[22] sts.
Work even until panel measures 16½[18]″ from beg, ending with a WS row.

Shape shoulder

Bind off 12 sts at beg of next row.
Purl one row.
Bind off rem 8[10] sts.

Back left panel

Work as for right side panel using B and reversing all shaping.

Front left panel

Using B, work as for back right panel from ** to **.
Cont in St st until panel measures 9¾[10¼]″ from beg, ending with a WS row.

Pocket placing

Next row K5[6] sts, bind off next 15 sts, K to end.
Next row P5[6] sts, cast on 15 sts, P to end.

Work even until panel measures same as back panels to armhole, ending with a WS row.

Shape armhole

Bind off 3 sts at beg of next row.
Dec one st at armhole edge on every other row twice. 20[22] sts.
Work even until panel measures 15[16¼]″ from beg, ending with a RS row.

Shape neck

Bind off 5[6] sts at beg of next row.
Knit one row.
Bind off 2[3] sts at beg of next row.
Knit one row.
Dec one st at beg of next row.
Cont in St st until panel measures same as back panels to shoulder.
Bind off rem 12 sts.

Front right panel

Using A, work as for front left panel, reversing all shaping.

Lower sleeves (make 2)

Using smaller needles and A, cast on 32[35] sts.
1st row K1, * P1, K1, rep from * to end.
2nd row P1, * K1, P1, rep from * to end.
Rep these 2 rows until sleeve measures 1½″ from beg.
Change to larger needles.
Next row K3[4], pick up strand between st just worked and next st and knit into back of it – called M1 –, *K2, M1, rep from * to last 3[5] sts, K3[5]. 46[49] sts.
Beg with a P row, work in St st until sleeve measures 6½[7¾]″ from beg.
Bind off.
Using B, make a 2nd lower sleeve in the same way.

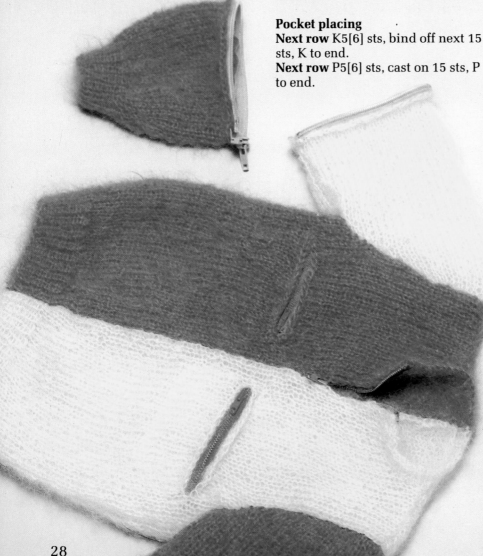

Upper sleeves (make 2)

Using larger needles and A, cast on
46[49] sts. Beg with a K row, work
in St st until sleeve measures
4[4¼]″ from beg, ending with a WS
row.

Shape cap

Bind off 3 sts at beg of next 2 rows.
40[43] sts.

Dec one st at beg of next row and
then on every other row until
20[23] sts rem.

Dec one st at beg of every row until
12[15] sts rem.

Bind off.

Using B, make a 2nd upper sleeve
in the same way.

Pocket linings (make 2)

Using larger needles and A, cast on
17 sts. Work in St st for 2½″
ending with a WS row.

Bind off.

Using B, make a 2nd pocket lining
in the same way.

Neckband

Each of back and front panels has a
neckband worked onto it separately
in a matching color. Using smaller
needles and with RS facing, pick
up and K9[11] sts for each of back
necks and 13[17] sts for each of
front necks.

Work in K1, P1 rib for 3 rows.

Bind off loosely in rib.

To finish

Join center front seam to within 4″
of top.

Join center back and shoulder
seams. Set in upper sleeves. Sew
side and upper sleeve seams.

Sew lower sleeve seams.

Attach open-ended zippers to
upper and lower halves of sleeves.
Sew red zippers to pocket
openings. Sew green zipper to neck
opening. Sew pocket linings to WS
of fronts.

HELPING HAND

Chain and slip stitch selvages

The edges of the knitted fabric that run up the right and left sides of the work are called the "selvages". In order to obtain neat selvages on stockinette stitch, it is necessary to work the first and last stitches of the row as firmly as possible. This is not always easy to do especially if you are a loose knitter. It is important to achieve even selvages on the bicolor top so that neat seams can be worked up the front and back of the garment. The chain selvage forms an edge which would be a suitable finish along the neck zipper. The slip stitch selvage is ideal for even seams.

Chain selvage

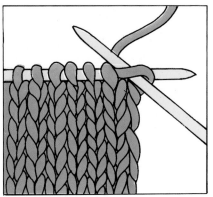

1 *On every knit row slip the first stitch knitwise. Knit in the ordinary way to the last stitch. Slip this stitch off the needle knitwise.*

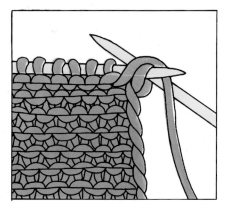

2 *On every purl row, purl every stitch. This forms a neat chain along the selvages.*

Slip stitch selvage

1 *On every knit row slip the first stitch knitwise, then knit to the end of the row.*

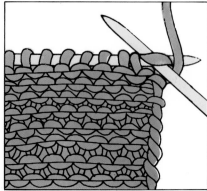

2 *On every purl row slip the first stitch knitwise, then purl to the last stitch and knit this stitch. A series of pips will be formed along the selvages. When working the seam, work into each pip.*

Ice Cream Sweater

Any child would be proud to wear this ice cream pullover. Work in pastel colors in a machine washable yarn. Top the cone with a cherry using the French knot technique.

Sizes

To fit 20[22:24]" chest
Length 12¼[13¾:17]"
Sleeve seam 7½[8¼:9¾]"
Note Instructions for larger sizes are in brackets [ ]; where there is only one set of figures it applies to all sizes.

Materials

☐ 4[4:5] oz of a sport weight yarn in main color MC (white)
☐ 1 oz in each of 6 contrasting colors A (turquoise), B (beige), C (light yellow), D (pink), E (light mint green) and F (peach)
☐ Small amount in red
☐ One pair each of sizes 2 and 3 knitting needles
☐ Size C crochet hook
☐ 2 small buttons
☐ Tapestry needle

Gauge

14 sts and 18 rows to 2" over St st using size 3 needles.

To save time, take time to check gauge.

Ice Cream Sweater

Back

***Using smaller needles and MC, cast on 76[82:90] sts. Work in K2, P2 rib for 12 rows.

Change to larger needles and beg with a K row, work in St st until back measures 6[7½:9½]" from beg, ending with a WS row.

Shape raglan armholes

Bind off 4 sts at beg of next 2 rows.
** **Next row** Using A, K2 tog, K to last 2 sts, K2 tog.
Next row Using A, K to end. **
Next row Using B, K2 tog, K1, * sl 1, K2, rep from * to last 3[3:2] sts, sl 1[1:0], K2 tog.
Next row Using B, P1[1:3], * sl 1, P2, rep from * to end.
Work from ** to ** once.
Beg with a K row, cont in St st and MC only, dec one st at each end of every other row until 34[42:48] sts rem, ending with a WS row.
Work from ** to ** once. ***
Next row Using B, K2 tog, K1[0:1], * sl 1, K2, rep from * to last 2[2:4] sts, sl 0[0:1], K0[0:1], K2 tog.
Next row Using B, P3[3:2], * sl 1, P2, rep from * to last 0[2:0] sts, sl 0[1:0], P0[1:0].
Work from ** to ** once.
Beg with a K row, cont in St st and MC only, dec one st at each end of every other row until 18[24:30] sts rem, ending with a WS row. Leave these sts on a spare needle.

Front

Work as for back from *** to ***.
Beg with a K row, cont in St st and MC only, dec one st at each end of every other row until 28[34:42] sts rem, ending with a WS row.

Neck shaping

Next row K2 tog, K8[8:10], turn.
Next row P2 tog, P to end.
Dec one st at armhole edge and neck edge on next row and then every other row until 2 sts rem. K2 tog and fasten off.

Shape second side of neck

Sl next 8[14:18] sts onto a stitch holder. Rejoin yarn to neck edge and work as for the first side, reversing the shaping.

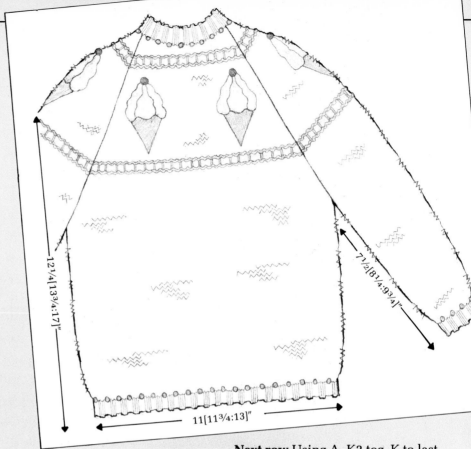

Sleeves (make 2)

Using smaller needles and MC, cast on 40[46:50] sts. Work 12 rows in K2, P2 rib.

Change to larger needles and beg with a K row, cont in St st, inc one st at each end of 3rd row and then every 6th row until there are 60 [66:70] sts.

Work even until sleeve measures 7½[8¼:9¾]" from beg, ending with a WS row.

Shape raglan top

Bind off 4 sts at beg of next 2 rows.
** **Next row** Using A, K2 tog, K to last 2 sts, K2 tog.
Next row Using A, K to end. **
Next row Using B, K2[2:1], * sl 1, K2, rep from * to last 0[0:2] sts, sl 0[0:1], K0[0:1].
Next row Using B, P2[2:1], * sl 1, P2, rep from * to last 0[2:2] sts, sl 0[0:1], P0[2:1].
Rep from ** to **. Beg with a K row, cont in St st and MC, dec one st at each end of every other row until 24[32:36] sts rem.

Next row Using A, K2 tog, K to last 2 sts, K2 tog.
Next row Using A, K to end.
Next row Using B, K2 tog, K1[2:1], * sl 1, K2, rep from * to last 4[2:4] sts, sl 1 [0:1], K1[0:1], K2 tog.
Next row Using B, P2[3:2], *sl 1, P2, rep from * to last 0[1:0]st, P0[1:0].
Next row Using A, K2 tog, K to last 2 sts, K2 tog.
Next row Using B, K to end.
Beg with a K row and using A, dec one at each end of every other row until 8[14:18] sts rem, ending with a WS row. Leave sts on a spare needle.

Neckband

Join all raglan seams, omitting right back seam.
With RS facing and using smaller needles and MC, K across 18[24:30] sts from back neck, 8[14:18] sts from left sleeve pick up and K5 sts down left neck, K across center 8[14:18] sts, pick up and K5 sts up right neck, then K across 8[14:18]

sts from right sleeve. 52[76:94] sts.
Work 8 rows in K2, P2 rib.
Bind off in rib.

To finish
Foll chart for embroidering the ice
cream cone motifs onto the yoke,
using duplicate st (see page 50).
Before beg, mark the positions of
the motifs with pins, leaving two
rows of A free above the stripe pat
before the end of the cones are
begun. Place two motifs across both
front and back yokes between two
stripes. Place one motif in center of
top of each sleeve between two
stripes.
After completing the motifs, work a
French knot (see Helping Hand) in
red on top of each ice cream cone.
Work a row of French knots along
the top of every other rib (purl st
ribs) on all ribbing, using C, D and
E alternately.
Join raglan seams leaving approx 3″
of back right seam open. Crochet
one row of single crochet (see page
161) along this opening, making
two chain loops for buttons.
Join side and sleeve seams.
Sew on buttons.

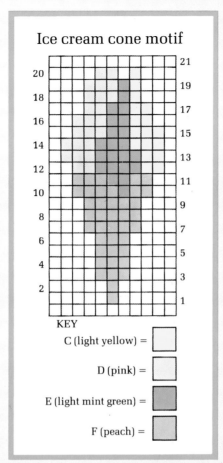

Ice cream cone motif

KEY

C (light yellow) =
D (pink) =
E (light mint green) =
F (peach) =

HELPING HAND

Making a French knot
When pulling the needle through,
the yarn wrapped around it, hold
the tip of the needle gently in the
left hand to keep the yarn in place.
For large knots use the yarn double
or increase the number of times the
yarn is wrapped around the needle.
Secure the yarn at the back of the
work and pass needle to front of
work. With the right side facing,
insert the needle under one knitted
loop, wind yarn loosely around the
needle four times and pull through
tightly. Pass needle through to back
of work at base of knot just made.

Sheep Vest

A shaggy sheep motif knitted in bouclé wool turns an ordinary vest into something very special. Tussocks of grass are worked in knotted tufts onto the knitted front for an extra touch of realism.

Size
To fit 24″ chest
Length 13″

Materials
☐ 8oz of a bulky weight yarn in main color MC (blue)
☐ 1¾ oz of a medium weight bouclé A (cream)
☐ Small amounts of a bulky weight yarn in 2 colors B (cream) and C (green)
☐ Small amount of fingering yarn in blue and size 2 needles for bobble
☐ One pair each of sizes 9 and 10½ knitting needles
☐ Crochet hook for tufts

Gauge
14 sts and 19 rows to 4″ over St st using size 10½ needles.

To save time, take time to check gauge.

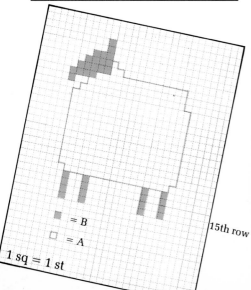

= B
☐ = A
15th row
1 sq = 1 st

Back

Using smaller needles and MC, cast on 46 sts. Work in K1, P1 rib for 8 rows.

Change to larger needles and work in St st for 32 rows.

Shape armholes

41st row Bind off 4 sts, K to end.
42nd row Bind off 4 sts, P to end.
43rd row K2 tog, K to last 2 sts, K2 tog.
44th row P2 tog, P to last 2 sts, P2 tog.
Rep 43rd and 44th rows once. 30 sts.
Cont in St st for 20 rows.

Shape shoulders

Bind off 3 sts at beg of next 4 rows.
Sl rem 18 sts onto a st holder.

Front

Work as for back for 14 rows.
Cont as for back, foll chart for sheep, centering the motif, and work to beg of armhole shaping.

Shape armholes

Cont to foll chart for sheep, shape armholes as for back.
Work 12 rows even after armhole shaping is completed.

Shape neck

59th row K11, sl 19 rem sts onto a st holder.
Working left side of neck first, bind off 2 sts at beg of next row.
Dec one st at neck edge on every row 3 times. 6 sts.
Work even until front measures same as back to shoulder.
Shape shoulder as for back.
Slip 8 center front sts onto a stitch holder and work 2nd side of neck as for first side, reversing the shaping.

Neckband

Join left shoulder seam.
With RS facing and using smaller needles and MC, K18 sts from back neck, pick up and K9 sts down left neck edge, K8 sts from center front neck, pick up and K9 sts up right front. 44 sts. Work 3 rows in K1. P1 rib.
Bind off loosely in rib.

Armbands

Joint right shoulder and neckband seam. With RS facing and using smaller needles and MC pick up and K56 sts along armhole edge.
Work 3 rows in K1, P1 rib.
Bind off loosely in rib.

To finish

Join side seams.
Using fingering yarn and size 2 needles, make a bobble for sheep's eye (see Helping Hand).
Make grass tufts with C cut into 2″ lengths. Take three strands tog and fold in half to form a loop. Insert crochet hook around a knit st below sheep and draw loop through. Draw ends through loop and pull tightly to secure knot. Work tufts at random as desired. Trim ends.
Press seams lightly on WS with warm iron.

HELPING HAND

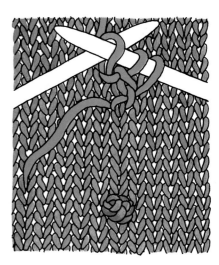

Making fringe

Fringe can be used to form an edging as on scarves or single fringe knots can be used to form decorate tufts as for grass of the sheep vest.
Begin by cutting several lengths of yarn. Hold the lengths together and fold in half to form a loop. Insert a crochet hook through the fabric at the position where the fringe knot is to be worked. Draw the loop through the knitted fabric. Then draw the ends through the loop on hook. Pull tightly to secure the knot. Trim ends if desired.

Applying bobbles

Bobbles, in matching or contrasting colors, can easily be applied to a knitted fabric. For small bobble use small needles and a fine yarn.

To make a bobble, with right side of work facing, insert a crochet hook into the center of chosen stitch. Wrap the yarn around the crochet hook and pull through to make a loop. Slip loop onto knitting needle and hold in your left hand. Knit into the front, back and front of the loop to make three stitches, turn, purl three stitches, turn and knit two stitches together, bind off one stitch and fasten off the remaining stitch. Darn in ends at back of work.

Slipstitch Top

Create a stunning slipstitch top, using the waffle pattern shown here or any of the other six slipstitch variations.

Size
To fit 28″ chest
Length 17¾″

Materials
☐ 9oz of a sport weight yarn in main color MC
☐ 3½oz in each of 2 contrasting colors A and B
☐ One pair each of sizes 3 and 6 knitting needles

Gauge
24 sts and 38 rows to 4″ over waffle pat using size 6 needles.

To save time, take time to check gauge.

Back
Using smaller needles and MC, cast on 79 sts. Beg and ending with a K st on RS rows, work in K1, P1 rib for 2″, ending with a WS row.
Next row Rib 2, pick up strand between st just worked and next st and work into back of it – called M1 –, *rib 5, M1, rep from * to last 2 sts, rib 2. 95 sts.
Change to larger needles and work in waffle slipstitch pat (see page 37) until back measures 10¾″ from beg, ending with a WS row.
Shape sleeves
Keeping pat correct, cast on 20 sts at beg of next 2 rows. 135 sts.
Cont in pat until back measures 17¾″ from beg, ending with a WS row.
Shape shoulders
Bind off 50 sts at beg of next 2 rows. Leave rem 35 sts on a st holder.

Front
Work as for back until front measures 13¾″ from beg, ending with a WS row.
Shape neck
Next row Work 57 sts in pat, work 2 tog, turn and leave rem sts on a st holder.
Complete left side of neck first.
Cont in pat on first 58 sts, dec one st at neck edge on next 4 rows, then dec one on every other row 4 times. 50 sts.
Cont in pat until front measures same as back as shoulder shaping, ending at armhole edge. Bind off.
With RS facing, sl center 17 sts onto a st holder. Rejoin yarn to rem 59 sts, work 2 tog, work in pat to end.
Complete to match left side of neck, reversing shaping.

Neckband
Join right shoulder seam.
With RS facing and using smaller needles and MC, pick up and K22 sts down left side of neck, K across 17 sts at center front, pick up and K22 sts up right side of neck, then K across 35 sts from back, dec one st at center. 96 sts. Work in K1, P1 rib as for back for ¾″
Bind off loosely in rib.

Armbands
Join left shoulder and neckband seams.
With RS facing and using smaller needles and MC, pick up and K60 sts around armhole edge.
Work in K1, P1 rib for ¾″
Bind off loosely in rib.

To finish
Join side, sleeve and armband seams.
Press seams lightly on WS with warm iron.

VARIATIONS
Any of these multicolored slipstitch patterns can be used for the top pictured. Stitch multiples are given for each of the patterns. Waffle pattern, shadow box, striped check, Navajo stitch and pinnacle stitch can all be worked over the 95 stitches of the back. For surprise pattern increase 2 extra stitches in the rib to begin the back with 97 stitches. Work woven check over 93 stitches. Remember to adjust the yarn quantities if the number of colors differs from that of the basic pattern.

1 Waffle pattern

This pat is worked over a multiple of 10 sts, plus 5 extra, and in 3 colors, (MC, A and B). Slip all sts with yarn on WS.

1st row (RS) With MC, K to end.

2nd row With MC, (P1, K1) twice, *P2, K1, P1, K1, rep from * to last 6 sts, P2, (K1, P1) twice.

3rd row With A, K5, *(sl 1, K1) twice, sl 1, K5, rep from * to end.

4th row With A, K5, *(sl, 1, K1) twice, sl 1, K5, rep from * to end.

5th row With MC, K to end.

6th row With MC, K5, *(P1, K1) twice, P1, K5, rep from * to end.

7th-10th rows As 3rd-6th rows.

11th-12th rows As 3rd-4th rows.

13th-14th rows As first-2nd rows.

15th row With B, (sl 1, K1) twice, sl 1, *K5, (sl 1, K1) twice, sl 1, rep from * to end.

16th row With B, (sl 1, K1) twice, sl 1, *K5, (sl 1, K1) twice, sl 1, rep from * to end.

17th row As 5th row.

18th row With B, (P1, K1) twice, P1, *K5, (P1, K1) twice, P1, rep from * to end.

19th-20th rows As 15th-16th rows.

21st row As 5th row.

22nd row As 18th row.

23rd row As 15th row.

24th row As 16th row.

These 24 rows form pat and are rep throughout.

2

3

4

2 Surprise pattern
This pat is worked over a multiple of 4 sts, plus 1 extra, and in 5 colors (A, B, C, D and E). Slip all sts with yarn on WS.
1st row (WS) With A, P to end.
2nd row With B, K2, *sl 1, K3, rep from * to last 3 sts, sl 1, K2.
3rd row With B, P2, *sl 1, P3, rep from * to last 3 sts, sl 1, P2.
4th row With C, K4, *sl 1, K3, rep from * to last st, K1.
5th row With C, P4, *sl 1, P3, rep from * to last st, P1.
6th row With A, K1, *sl 1, K1, rep from * to end.
7th row With A, P to end.
8th row With D, K2, *sl 1, K1, rep from * to last st, K1.
9th row With D, P4, *sl 1, P3, rep from * to last st, P1.
10th row With E, K2, *sl 1, K3, rep from * to last 3 sts, sl 1, K2.
11th row With E, P to end.
12th row With A, K1, *sl 1, K1, rep from * to end.
These 12 rows form pat and are rep throughout.

3 Shadow box
This pat is worked over a multiple of 4 sts, plus 3 extra, and in 3 colors (A, B and C). Slip all sts with yarn on WS.
1st row (RS) With A, K to end.
2nd row With A, K1, * K1 winding yarn twice around needle, K3, rep from *, ending last rep K1 instead of K3.
3rd row With B, K1, * sl 1 dropping extra loops, K3, rep from *, ending last rep K1 instead of K3.
4th row With B, K1, *sl 1, K3, rep from * to last 2 sts, sl 1, K1.
5th row With C, K1, *sl 2, K2, rep from * to last 2 sts, sl 1, K1.
6th row With C, K1, sl 1, *P2, sl 2, rep from * to last st, K1.
These 6 rows form pat and are rep throughout.

4 Striped check
This pat is worked over a multiple of 4 sts, plus 3 extra, and in 4 colors (A, B, C and D). Slip all sts with yarn on WS. Cast on with D.
1st row (RS) With A, K1, *sl, K3, rep from * to last 2 sts, sl 1, K1.
2nd row With A, P1, *sl 1, P3, rep from * to last 2 sts, sl 1, K1.
3rd row With B, *K3, sl 1, rep from * to last 3 sts, K3.
4th row With B, *P3, sl 1, rep from * to last 3 sts, P3.
5th-6th rows With C, as first-2nd rows.
7th-8th rows With D, as 3rd-4th rows.
These 8 rows form pat and are rep throughout.

6

5

7

5 Navajo stitch
This pat is worked over a
multiple of 4 sts, plus 3 extra,
and in 3 colors (A, B, C).
1st row (RS) With A, K to end.
2nd row With A, P to end.
3rd row With B, K1, *yarn to
front of work, sl 1, yarn to back
of work – called sl 1 with yarn in
front (wyif) –, K1, rep from * to
end.
4th row With B, P to end.
5th row With A, K2, *sl 1 wyif,
K1, rep from * to last st, K1.
6th row With A, P to end.
7th and 9th rows With C, K1,
*sl 1 with yarn in back (wyib),
ending last rep, K1 instead of K3.
8th and 10th rows With C, P1, *
sl 1 wyif, P3, rep from *, ending
last rep P1.
These 10 rows form pat and are
rep throughout.

6 Pinnacle stitch
This pat is worked over a
multiple of 4 sts, plus 3 extra,
and in 4 colors (A, B, C and D).
Slip all sts with yarn on WS.
1st row (WS) With A, K1, P to
last st, K1.
2nd row With B, K2, *sl 1, K1,
rep from * to last st, K1.
3rd row With B, K1, P1, *sl 1,
P1, rep from * to last st, K1.
4th row With C, K1, *sl 1, K1,
rep from * to end.
5th row With C, K1, P to last st, K1.
6th row With D, K1, *sl 1, K3,
rep from * to last 2 sts, sl 1, K1.
7th row With D, K1, *sl 1, P3,
rep from * to last 2 sts, sl 1, K1.
8th row With B, K2, *sl 3, K1,
rep from * to last st, K1.
9th row With B, K1, P2, *sl 1,
P3, rep from * to last 4 sts, sl 1,
P2, K1.
10th row With A, as 6th row.
These 10 rows form pat and are
rep throughout.

7 Woven check
This pat is worked over a
multiple of 8 sts, plus 5 extra,
and in 3 colors (A, B and C). Cast
on with C.
1st row (WS) P to end.
2nd row With A, K5, *yarn to
back of work – called ybk –, sl 1,
yarn to front – called yft –, sl 1,
ybk, sl 1, K5, rep from * to end.
3rd row With A, K1, P3, K1, *
yft, sl 1, ybk, sl 1, yft, sl 1, ybk,
K1, P3, K1, rep from * to end.
4th row With B, K1, *ybk, sl 1,
yft, sl 1, ybk, sl 1, K5, rep from *,
ending last rep K1 instead of K5.
5th row With B, K1, *yft, sl 1,
ybk, sl 1, yft, sl 1, ybk, K1, P3,
K1, rep from * to last 4 sts, yft, sl
1, ybk, sl 1, yft, sl 1, ybk, K1.
6th-7th rows With C, as 2nd-3rd
rows.
8th-9th rows With A, as 4th-5th
rows.
10th-11th rows With B, as 2nd-
3rd rows.
12th-13th rows With C, as 4th-
5th rows.
The 2nd-13th rows form pat and
are rep throughout.

Vest with Pockets

Any boy or girl would love to wear this simple ribbed vest with pockets. Work all the edgings in a contrasting color and choose bright buttons to fasten.

Size
To fit 25-27″ chest
Length 15¾″

Materials
- ☐ 6oz of a sport weight yarn in main color MC
- ☐ 1¾oz in contrasting color A
- ☐ 5 buttons
- ☐ One pair each of size 3 and 7 knitting needles

Gauge
30 sts and 25 rows to 4″ over rib pat on size 7 needles.

To save time, take time to check gauge.

Back
Using smaller needles and A, cast on 85 sts.
1st row K1, * P1, K1, rep from * to end.
2nd row P1, * K1, P1, rep from * to end.
Rep last 2 rows twice more. Change to larger needles and MC and cont in rib pat until back measures 8″ from beg, ending with a WS row.
Shape armholes
Bind off 4 sts at beg of next 2 rows. Dec one st at beg of next row and then every other row until there are 65 sts.
Work even until back measures 15¾″ from beg, ending with a WS row.
Shape shoulder
Bind off 15 sts at beg of next 2 rows.
Neck edge
Change to smaller needles and A and work 4 rows in rib.
Bind off in rib.

Pocket linings (make 2)
Using larger needles and MC, cast on 16 sts. Work in K1, P1 rib for 18 rows. Leave these sts on a st holder.

Left front
Using smaller needles and A, cast on 40 sts. Work in K1, P1 rib for 6 rows.
Change to larger needles and MC and cont in rib until front measures 6″ from beg, ending with a WS row.
Pocket placing
Next row Rib 12, sl next 16 sts onto a st holder, work across 16 sts of pocket lining, work to end of row. Work one row.
Shape neck
Dec one st at beg of next row and then every 4th row until front measures 8″ from beg, ending with a WS row.
Shape armhole
Bind off 4 sts at beg of next row. Work one row.
Dec one st at beg of next row and then every other row until 30 sts rem, and *at the same time* cont dec at neck edge until 15 sts rem.
Work even on these 15 sts until front measures 15¾″ from beg, ending with a WS row. Bind off.

Pocket edgings
With RS facing and using smaller

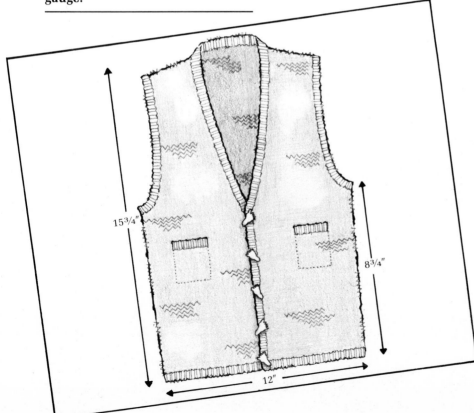

needles and A, K across 16 sts on holder, inc one st at each end.
Work in K1, P1 rib for 4 rows.
Bind off.
Sew edgings in place.

Buttonband
With RS facing and using smaller needles and MC, beg at cast-on edge and pick up and K84 sts up front.
Using A, work 5 rows in K1, P1 rib.

Bind off loosely in rib.

Buttonhole band
With RS facing and using smaller needles and MC, beg at shoulder and pick up and K84 sts down front.
Using A, work 3 rows in rib.
Buttonhole row Rib 4, yo, K2 tog, * rib 8, yo, K2 tog, rep from * 3 times, rib to end.
Next row Rib to end.
Bind off loosely in rib.

Armbands
Join shoulder seams.
With RS facing and using smaller needles and MC, pick up and K90 sts along armhole edge.
Using A, work 5 rows in rib.
Bind off loosely in rib.

To finish
Join side and neckband seams.
Sew in pocket linings.
Sew on buttons.

HELPING HAND

Making pockets
Pocket linings are worked separately before the fronts are begun. They are not bound off but are left on a stitch holder ready to be knitted into the main fabric when the pocket position is reached.

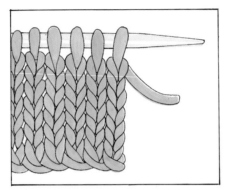

1 Work the pocket lining first as instructed in your pattern. When the lining is completed leave the stitches on a stitch holder.

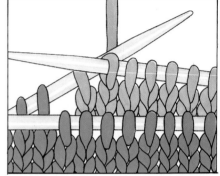

2 Work to position of pocket on the garment and slip as many stitches used for the pocket lining onto a stitch holder and leave at the front of work. Work across the lining stitches; work to end of row.

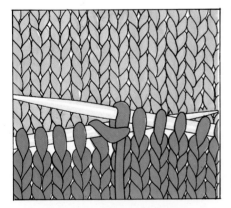

3 When the main section of the garment has been completed, rejoin the yarn to the pocket stitches on the stitch holder. Increase one stitch at each end of first row to avoid holes when making up the garment.

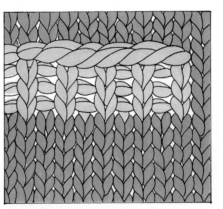

4 Work in rib across these stitches for the desired depth. Bind off loosely in rib.

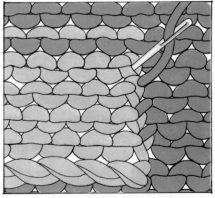

5 On the wrong side, sew the pocket lining in place. The stitching should not show on the right side of the fabric. Sew the pocket edging to the right side.

Striped Pullover

This boatneck pullover is quickly and easily made, as all the pattern pieces are rectangles and the sleeves and neck require no shaping.

Sizes
To fit 22[23:24]″ chest
Length 11[13:15]″
Sleeve seam 9½[11:12½]″
Note Instructions for larger sizes are in brackets [ ]; where there is only one set of figures it applies to all sizes.

Materials
- ☐ 3½ oz of a sport weight yarn in main color (MC)
- ☐ 1¾ oz in each of 2 contrasting colors A and B
- ☐ 1¾[1¾:3½] oz in contrasting color C
- ☐ One pair each of sizes 5 and 6 knitting needles
- ☐ 2 buttons
- ☐ Size G crochet hook

Gauge
22 sts and 30 rows to 4″ over St st using size 6 needles.

To save time, take time to check gauge.

Note To avoid having to weave in lots of loose ends do not break the yarn when a stripe is completed, but carry the yarns up the right-hand side of the work. Do not let the ends of the yarn become tangled.

Striped Pullover

Back
Using smaller needles and MC, cast on 66[69:72] sts. K 9 rows.
Change to larger needles and beg stripe pat as foll:
*Beg with a K row and using A, work 2 rows in St st. Cont in St st, work 4 rows using B. Using MC, K 2 rows. Beg with a K row and using C, work 8 rows in St st. Cont in St st, work 6 rows using MC.
These 22 rows from * form stripe pat. Cont in stripe pat until back measures 10¼[12¼:14¼]" from beg, ending with a P row.
K 6 rows, either in stripe pat as before, or all in one of the colors. Bind off loosely.

Front
Work as for back.

Sleeves (make 2)
Using smaller needles and MC, cast on 50[55:61] sts.
Work as for back until sleeve measures 9½[11:12½]" from beg. Bind off loosely.

To finish
Join bound-off edges of back and front, leaving center 6¾[7:7½]" open for neck.
Placing center of bound-off edge of sleeve at shoulder seam, sew on sleeves. Join side and sleeve seams. On bound-off edge of front, make a button loop ½" from the inner end of each shoulder seam as foll: Using crochet hook and same color yarn as last stripe, make two lengths of chain each long enough to fit over button (see Helping Hand). Leave a long end at each end of chain. Using long ends sew loops to front neck edge.
Sew on buttons to back neck edge. opposite loops.

HELPING HAND

Making a crochet chain
Like knitting, crochet begins with a simple slip loop. The simplest stitch in crochet is a chain stitch and a series of chain stitches are called "a length of chain."

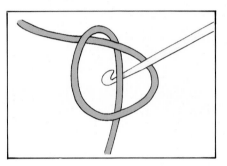

1 *Make a loop near the end of the yarn. Insert the tip of the hook through the loop and, catching the yarn with the hook, pull the yarn back through the loop. Pull tightly to secure the knot. This does not count as a stitch.*

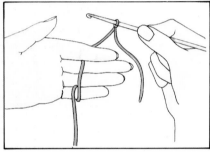

2 *Hold the hook in your right hand as you would a pencil, with middle and first fingers near the tip. Wrap the yarn from the ball around your left hand loosely, as shown.*

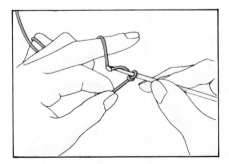

3 *Hold the loose end of the yarn between the thumb and forefinger of the left hand. Insert the hook under then over the taut yarn. This is called "yarn over hook".*

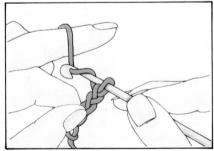

4 *Draw the caught yarn through the loop on the hook. This makes one chain. Repeat for required number of chains. To fasten off, break off the yarn, draw the end through the loop on the hook and pull to secure.*

Train Vest

Any remnants of bright colored cotton fabric can be used to work the appliqué train set. Once all the pieces have been ironed onto the vest, work the embroidery stitches to finish off the picture.

Sizes
To fit 22[24:26]″ chest
Length 13¼[14¾:16]″
Note Instructions for larger sizes are in brackets [ ]; where there is only one set of figures it applies to all sizes.

Materials
☐ 6[6:7] oz of a sport yarn in main color MC (blue)
☐ Small amount of lightweight fluffy yarn in A (white)
☐ Small amount of a sport yarn in B (navy)
☐ Small amounts of washable fabric in red, yellow, green and navy for appliqué
☐ One pair each of sizes 3 and 5 knitting needles
☐ One packet bonding fabric for appliqué

Gauge
24 sts and 32 rows to 4″ over St st using size 5 needles.

To save time, take time to check gauge.

Note The appliqué pieces are ironed onto the knitting using a bonding fabric. The yarn chosen should be able to be pressed. If it is not the pieces should be sewn to the knitting.

Train Vest

Back
Using smaller needles and MC, cast on 74[80:86] sts and work in K1, P1 rib for 1¼[1¼:1½]".
Change to size 5 needles and beg with a K row, work even in St st until back measures 8¼[9½:10¼]" from beg, ending with a P row.
Shape armholes
Bind off 4[5:6] sts at beg of next 2 rows. Dec one at each end of next 4 rows. 58[62:66] sts.
Work even in St st until armhole measures 5[5¼:5¾]", ending with a P row.
Shape shoulders
Bind off 6 sts at beg of next 4 rows. Bind off 5[6:7] sts at beg of next 2 rows. Leave rem 24[26:28] sts on a st holder.

Front
Work as for back until front measures 2 rows less than back to armholes, ending with a P row.
Divide for V-neck
Next row K35[38:41], K2 tog, turn and work on these sts, leaving rem sts on a st holder.
P one row.
Next row Bind off 4[5:6] sts, K to end.
Next row P2 tog, P to end.
Dec 1 st at armhole edge on next 4 rows, *at the same time* dec one st at neck edge on every 3rd row from previous dec until 26[28:30] sts rem.
Keeping armhole edge straight, dec one st at neck edge on every 3rd row until 17[18:19] sts rem.
Work even in St st until front measures same as back to shoulder, ending with a P row.

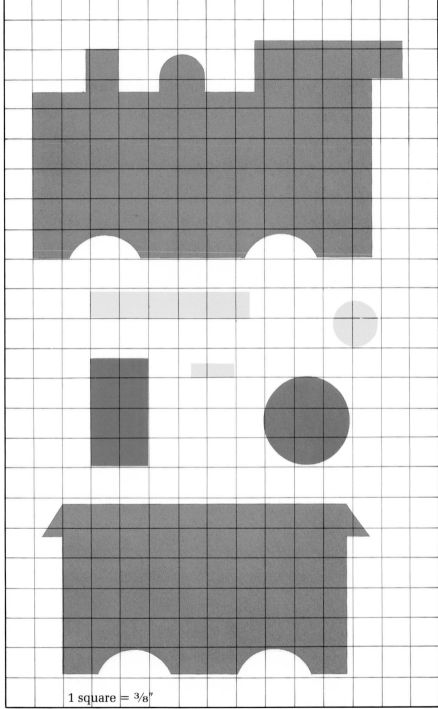

1 square = ⅜"

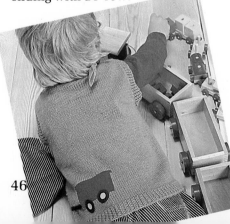

Shape shoulder
Bind off at armhole edge on every other row 6 sts twice and 5[6:7] sts once.
With RS facing, rejoin yarn to rem 37[40:43] sts.
Next row K2 tog, K to end.
Complete 2nd side of neck to match first side reversing all shaping.

Neckband
Join right shoulder seam.
With RS facing and using smaller needles and MC, pick up and K41[43:45] sts down left side of neck, pick up and K one st from center front and mark this st, pick up and K41[43:45] sts up right side of neck, K across 24[26:28] sts from back neck. 107[113:119] sts.
1st row (WS) * K1, P1, rep from * to within 2 sts of marked st, K2 tog, P marked st, K2 tog, then work in P1, K1 rib to end.
2nd row Rib to within 2 sts of marked st, P2 tog, K center st, P2 tog, rib to end.
Rep these 2 rows twice and first row again.
Bind off evenly in rib, dec as before.

Armbands
Join left shoulder seam and neckband.
With RS facing and using smaller needles and MC, pick up and K82[86:90] sts around edge of armhole.
Work 7 rows in K1, P1 rib. Bind off loosely in rib.

To finish
Press lightly on WS with warm iron. Join side seams.
Appliqué
Foll chart, draw train pieces onto graph paper enlarging to correct scale. Using remnants of washable fabric, trace off the train engine, two wagons, wheels, doors and panels onto bonding fabric, then iron the bonding to the back of the washable material. Cut out pieces. Remove paper backing and iron train engine, wagons and wheels in position as in photograph.
Embroidery
Using B double, embroider a chain stitch line (see page 163) between the train engine and wagons.
Using A, make three small fairly flat pompons (see page 127) and sew to front of vest to form puffs of billowing smoke.

HELPING HAND

Appliqué on knitting
A very simple and effective method of decorating a plain knitted garment is by adding appliqué. For this, motifs are cut out from a woven fabric and then sewn on or ironed onto the knitting using a bonding fabric. The bonding consists of a very fine web of adhesive fiber mounted onto a backing paper. It is semi-transparent, so motifs can be traced straight onto it. The bonding fuses to both fabrics when pressed. There are, however, a few commonsense guidelines which should always be followed. Check the yarn label that the knitting yarn used can be pressed and also check that the woven fabric is pre-shrunk and colorfast. Bonding appliqué should only be applied to a smooth surface such as stockinette stitch. As the bonding fabric is ironed onto the wrong side of the woven fabric remember to reverse the motif, if appropriate, as the wrong side of the motif will be facing. Motifs can also be stitched onto knitted fabrics, but this should be done by hand – preferably using embroidery silks or fine knitting yarn.

1 *Lay the bonding fabric over the pattern for the motif, paper side up. Trace the motifs with a pencil remembering to reverse the motifs if appropriate.*

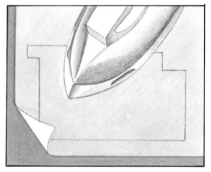

2 *With a hot iron, press the rough side of the bonding fabric to the wrong side of the motif fabric until the fibers are firmly stuck to the fabric.*

3 *Cut out the shapes with sharp scissors, following the pencil line carefully. Peel the paper backing away from each motif.*

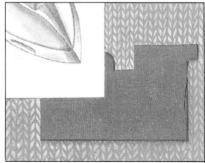

4 *Arrange the shapes on the knitting with the wrong side of motifs to right side of knitting. Cover with a damp cloth and press. Leave to cool.*

Chinese Motif Jacket

This toddler's jacket combines practical warmth and comfort with bold color and a traditional touch of the Orient. Take your pick from three motifs to embroider an individual emblem onto the back.

Size
To fit 22″ chest
Length 13¾″
Sleeve seam 7″

Materials
- ☐ 9oz of a bulky weight yarn in main color MC
- ☐ 1½oz in a contrasting color A
- ☐ One pair of size 10 knitting needles
- ☐ Two snaps
- ☐ Tapestry needle

Gauge
12 sts and 16 rows to 4″ over St st using size 10 needles.

To save time, take time to check gauge.

Note The sweater shown here is embroidered with the "water" motif. If you choose to use one of the other motifs follow the charts provided. For the plum blossom motif small amounts of two extra contrasting colors are required.

Back
Using A, cast on 38 sts. Work in garter st (K every row) for 4 rows. Using MC and beg with a K row, cont in St st until back measures 13¾″ from beg, ending with a P row.
Shape shoulders
Bind off 6 sts at beg of next 4 rows. Leave rem 14 sts on a st holder for back neck.

Left front
Using A, cast on 19 sts. Work in garter st for 4 rows.
Next row (RS) K16 MC, K3 A.
Next row K3 A, P16 MC.
Cont in this way, working a garter st border in A until front measures 11½″ from beg, ending with WS row.
Shape neck
Next row Using MC, K14, K2 tog, turn and leave rem 3 A sts on a st holder.
** Cont in St st, dec one st at neck edge on every row until 12 sts rem. Work even until front measures same as back to shoulder, ending at armhole edge.
Shape shoulder
Next row Bind off 6 sts, work to end.
Work one row.
Bind off rem 6 sts.**

Right front
Using A, cast on 25 sts.
Work in garter st for 4 rows.
Next row (RS) K3 A, K22 MC.

Next row P22 MC, K3 A.
Rep these 2 rows until front measures 8½″ from beg, ending with a WS row.
Shape neck
Next row K3 A, using MC, K2 tog, K to end.
Next row Using MC, P to last 3 sts, K3 A.
Rep last 2 rows until 19 sts rem, ending with a WS row.
Next row K3 A and leave these sts on a st holder, using MC, K2 tog, K to end.
Complete to match left front, working from ** to **.

Sleeves (make 2)
Using A, cast on 26 sts. Work in garter st for 4 rows.
Using MC and beg with a K row, cont in St st, inc one st at each end of next row and then every 4th row until there are 38 sts.
Work even until sleeve measures 7″ from beg.
Bind off.

Neckband
Join shoulder seams.
With RS facing, sl 3 sts from right front st holder onto needle, join in A and pick up and K8 sts up right side neck, K14 sts across back neck, pick up and K8 sts down left side neck, K3 sts across left front st holder. 36 sts.
Work in garter st for 2 rows.
Next row K2 tog, K to end.
Rep last row 3 times more. Bind off.

To finish
Using tapestry needle, embroider chosen motif in center of back in duplicate st (see page 50).
Mark 6″ down from shoulder seams on back and front, and sew bound-off edge of sleeves between these points.
Join side and sleeve seams.
Place right over left front to a line 6 sts from left front garter st edge.
Sew on snaps, the first to come at beg of neck shaping on right front with the other 4″ below.

Chinese frogging (make 3)
To make T-shape cut 2 lengths of A: one 8¾″ long and one 11″ long. Double longer length and knot twice at doubled end to form button. Slip stitch length tog for 1¼″. Slip stitch ends tog to form circles.
Work shorter length as for knotted length but form loop instead of knot.
Sew to coat, placing one at neck and others over snaps to give a neat finish.

HELPING HAND

Working duplicate stitch
Duplicate stitch is a form of embroidery which is worked on a stockinette stitch background and "duplicates" the knit stitch. It gives the impression that the design has been knitted in. It can be used for any design that is given in a chart form.

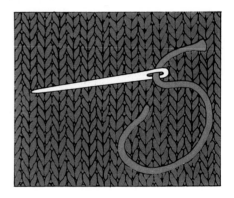

1 *Thread a large blunt-ended tapestry needle and secure the yarn at the back of the work. Bring the needle to the front of the work at the bottom of the stitch.*

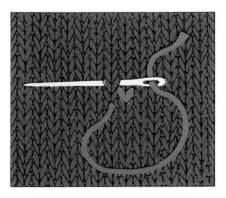

2 *Insert the needle through the top of the same stitch, tracing the path of the stitch. Pull yarn through and insert the needle through the same place at the base, bringing it through at the base of the next stitch.*

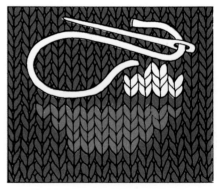

3 *Continue in this way, tracing the path of a row of knit stitches. Each background stitch should be completely covered by the embroidery stitch.*

VARIATIONS

Here are three oriental motifs to choose from to decorate the back of the jacket. Before beginning the embroidery, find the center of the motif and of the back in order to position the motif.

Plum blossom

The Japanese are renowned for their beautiful gardens full of flowering shrubs and trees which, in turn, inspired the designs and motifs of artists and craftsmen. This motif is worked over 24 stitches and 28 rows.

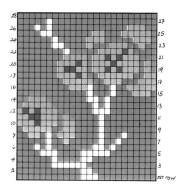

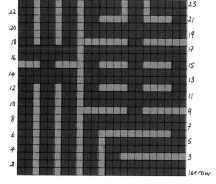

Water

This is a Chinese character meaning "water". It is worked over 24 stitches and 33 rows.

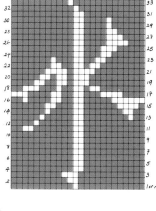

Badge

Traditional Japanese costume was often marked with the family crest or emblem of the wearer. On the clothes of the wealthy these could be elaborate, but more often than not they were bold, easily recognisable devices like this one. The motif is worked over 23 stitches and 23 rows.

51

Christmas Tree Sweater

Knit this neat "Christmas tree" sweater for the smaller branches of your family tree. It's bound to prove popular in the festive season.

Sizes
To fit 26[28:30]" chest
Length 14¼[15½:17¼]"
Sleeve seam 13[14¼:15¼]"
Note Instructions for larger sizes are in brackets [ ]; where there is only one set of figures it applies to all sizes.

Materials
☐ 7[7:9] oz of a sport weight yarn in main color MC
☐ 1¾ oz in each of 2 contrasting colors A and B
☐ One pair each of sizes 3 and 5 knitting needles
☐ Set of four size 3 double-pointed knitting needles
☐ Red beads and gold sequins (optional)

Gauge
24 sts and 32 rows to 4" over St st using size 5 needles.

To save time, take time to check gauge.

Back
** Using smaller needles and MC, cast on 85[91:97] sts. Work in K1, P1 rib as foll:
1st row K1, *P1, K1, rep from * to end.

2nd row P1, *K1, P1, rep from * to end.
Rep last 2 rows until rib measures 1½" from cast-on edge, ending with a 2nd row and inc one st at

center of last row. 86[92:98] sts. Change to larger needles and beg with a K row, cont in St st.
Work even for 4 rows.
Beg working from chart, noting that the motif is worked in garter st (K every row) on St st background, as foll:
***1st row** K7[7:8] MC, *K2 A, K12[14:14] MC, K2 A, K12[12:14] MC*, rep from * to * once, K2 A, K12[14:14] MC, K2 A, K7[7:8] MC.
2nd row P7[7:8] MC, *K2 A, P12[14:14] MC, K2 A, P12[12:14] MC*, rep from * to * once, K2 A, P12[14:14] MC, K2 A, P7[7:8] MC.
These 2 rows establish the position of the first line of tree motifs.
Beg with 3rd row, cont to work from chart for 10 rows.
Next row *K2 A, K12[13:14] MC, rep from * to last 2 sts, K2 A.
This row establishes the position of the second line of tree motifs. Beg with 2nd row, cont to work from chart for 11 rows.
Cont in MC only and St st until back measures 7[7¾:8½]" from beg, ending with a P row.
Beg to work from *** again, work even for 10 rows.
Shape armholes
Keeping pat correct, bind off 4 sts at beg of next 2 rows.
Next row K1 MC, K2 MC tog, K7[8:9] MC, *K2 A, K12[13:14] MC*, rep from * to * 3 times more, K2 A, with MC K7[8:9], sl 1-K1-psso, K1.
Next row Work in pat to end.
Keeping pat correct, cont to dec in this way one st at each end of next row and then every other row until 68[74:80] sts rem.
Work even until second line of trees is completed.**
Cont in MC only and St st until back measures 6[6½:7½]" from

beg of armhole shaping, ending with a P row.
Shape shoulders
Bind off 5[6:6] sts at beg of next 6 rows and 6[5:7] sts at beg of next 2 rows. Leave rem 26[28:30] sts on a st holder.

Front
Work as for back from ** to **.
Cont in MC only and St st until front measures 4[4¼:4¾]" from beg of armhole shaping, ending with a P row.
Shape neck
Next row K27[29:31] and turn, leaving rem sts on a st holder.
Complete left side of neck first as foll:
Bind off at neck edge on every other row 2 sts twice. Then dec one st at neck edge on every other row twice. 21[23:25] sts.
Work even until front matches back to shoulder, ending at armhole edge.
Shape shoulder
Bind off at armhole edge on every other row 5[6:6] sts 3 times and 6[5:7] sts once.
With RS facing, return to sts on st holder.
Sl center 14[16:18] sts onto a st holder, join in MC to next st and K to end.
Next row P to end.
Complete to match first side of neck, reversing shaping.

Sleeves (make 2)
Using smaller needles and MC, cast on 37[39:41] sts. Work in K1, P1 rib as for back for 2", ending with a 2nd row and inc 9 sts evenly across last row. 46[48:50] sts.
Change to larger needles and beg working from chart as foll:
1st row K22[23:24] MC, K2 A, K22[23:24] MC.
This row establishes the position of one tree motif. Beg with 2nd row, cont to work from chart for 11 rows and rep these 12 rows throughout, *at the same time* inc one st at each end of 3rd row and then every 8th

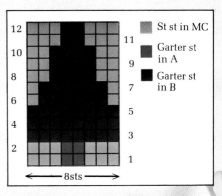

row until there are 68[72:76] sts.
Work even in pat until sleeve measures approx 13[14¼:15¼]" from beg, ending with a 4th[2nd:12th] pat row.
Shape cap
Keeping pat correct, bind off 4 sts at beg of next 2 rows.
Next row K1, K2 tog, work in pat to last 3 sts, sl 1-K1-psso, K1.
Next row Work in pat to end.
Rep last 2 rows until 44[46:48] sts rem, ending with a 2nd row.
Bind off 2 sts at beg of next 10 rows and 3 sts at beg of next 4 rows.
Bind off rem 12[14:16] sts.

Neckband
Join shoulder seams.
Using three of the set of double-pointed needles and MC and with RS facing, K26[28:30] sts across back neck, pick up and K22[24:26] sts down left side of neck, K across 14[16:18] sts at center front, pick up and K22[24:26] sts up right side of neck. 84[92:100] sts.
Using fourth needle, work in rounds of K1, P1 rib for 2½".
Bind off loosely in rib.

To finish
Press lightly on WS with warm iron.
Join side and sleeve seams. Set in sleeves.
Fold neckband in half onto WS and sew in place.
Sew on sequins and beads as shown, if desired.

Chart legend:
- St st in MC
- Garter st in A
- Garter st in B
- 8sts

Picot Top

The picot edging around the neck and armholes form a charming decoration on this simple and classic top. Knit it in a soft wool or a cotton yarn.

Sizes
To fit 20[22]″ chest or a one [two] year old child
Length 11¾[13½]″
Note Instructions for larger size are in brackets [ ]; where there is only one set of figures it applies to both sizes.

Materials
☐ 2[3] oz of a sport weight yarn
☐ One pair each of sizes 3 and 6 knitting needles
☐ 3 small buttons

Gauge
24 sts and 32 rows to 4″ over St st using size 6 needles.

To save time, take time to check gauge.

Back

* Using smaller needles, cast on 57[63] sts. Work in rib as foll:

1st row (RS) K1, * P1, K1, rep from * to end.

2nd row P1, * K1, P1, rep from * to end.

Rep last 2 rows until back measures 1¼" from beg, ending with a first row.

Inc row Rib 6, (pick up strand between st just worked and next st and work into back of it – called M1 –, rib 9[10]) 5 times, M1, rib to end. 63[69] sts.

Change to larger needles and beg with a K row, work in St st until back measures 7¾[8¾]" from beg, ending with a P row.

Shape armholes

Bind off 4 sts at beg of next 2 rows.

Dec one st at each end of every row 5[7] times.

Dec one st at each end of every other row until 39[43] sts rem, ending with P row. *

Divide for opening

Next row K18[20], turn and leave rem sts on a spare needle.

Cont in St st until armhole measures 4[4¾]" from beg, ending with a P row.

Shape shoulder

Bind off 6[7] sts at beg of next row.

Leave rem 12[13] sts on a spare needle.

Shape second side of neck

With RS facing, rejoin yarn to rem sts and bind off next 3 sts.

Complete as for first side, reversing all shaping.

Front

Work as for back from * to *.

Work even until armhole measures 2[2½]", ending with a P row.

Shape neck

Next row K13[15], turn and leave rem sts on a spare needle.

Next row P2 tog, P to end.

Keeping armhole edge straight, dec one st at neck edge on every row 3 more times.

Then dec one st on every other row until 6[7] sts rem.

Work even until front matches back to shoulder.

Bind off.

Shape second side of neck

With RS facing, rejoin yarn to rem sts and bind off center 13 sts loosely at beg of row.

Complete to match first side, reversing all shaping.

Neckband

Join right shoulder seam.

With RS facing and using smaller needles, K across 12[13] sts from left back neck, pick up and K39[43] sts around front neck, K across 12[13] sts from right back neck. 63[69] sts.

With RS facing, work 3 rows in St st.

Next row K1, * yo, K2 tog, rep from * to end.

Work 3 rows in St st, beg with a P row.

Bind off loosely.

Fold neckband in half to WS and sew in place.

Buttonhole band

With RS facing and using smaller needles, pick up and K20[26] sts down RS of back opening.

K one row.

Buttonhole row K1, * yo, K2 tog, K6[8], rep from * twice, yo, K2 tog, K1[3].

K 2 rows.

Bind off.

Button band

Work button band as for buttonhole band, omitting buttonholes.

Armbands

Join left shoulder seam.

With RS facing and using smaller needles, pick up K47[53] sts around edge of armhole.

Work as for neckband.

To finish

Join side seams and armbands.

Fold armbands to WS and sew in place.

Press lightly on WS with warm iron.

HELPING HAND

Working a picot edging

Picot edging is a delicate alternative to ribbing for armbands and neckbands. For a firm hem use smaller needles than the ones used for the main pieces of the garment.

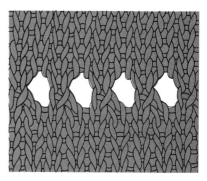

1 *With the right side facing, pick up an odd number of stitches around the neck edge or armhole. Work in stockinette stitch until the band is the desired depth, ending with a wrong side row. The eyelet holes form the foldline of the edge. To make the eyelet holes begin the row by * knitting two stitches together, bring the yarn to the front of work to form a yarn over. Repeat from * to the end of the row, knitting the last stitch. Beginning with a purl row, continue in stockinette stitch until one row less than the number of rows to the eyelet holes have been worked. Bind off loosely.*

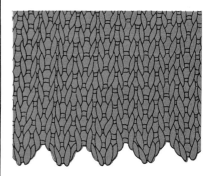

2 *When finishing, turn the hem to the wrong side along eyelet hole row and sew in place.*

Beach Pullover

Any little girl would love to wear this appliquéd jumper. Remnants of fabric, ribbon and lace are used to create the simple fishing motif and trim the neck and armbands.

Sizes
To fit 24[26:28]" chest
Length 14¼[15¾:17¼]"
Sleeve seam 11½[12¼:13¾]"
Note Instructions for larger sizes are in brackets [ ]; where there is only one set of figures it applies to all sizes.

Materials
☐ 7[7:9] oz of a sport weight yarn
☐ One pair each of sizes 3 and 5 knitting needles
☐ Set of four size 3 double-pointed knitting needles
☐ 4 small buttons
☐ Remnants of fabric, ribbon and lace
☐ Small amount of navy sport yarn and white fingering yarn
☐ Small piece of lightweight iron-on interfacing
☐ Fabric tracing paper

Gauge
23 sts and 30 rows to 4" over St st using size 5 needles.

To save time, take time to check gauge.

Note When choosing the fabrics, be careful to use ones which wash easily, such as a cotton. If desired, the shapes can be folded over and hemmed neatly before being sewn onto the actual garment.

Back
** Using smaller needles, cast on 71[77:83] sts. Work in rib as foll:
1st row (RS) K1, * P1, K1, rep from * to end.
2nd row P1, * K1, P1, rep from * to end.
Rep last 2 rows for 2½", ending with a first row.
Inc row Rib 8[8:7], (pick up strand between st just worked and next st and work into back of it – called M1 –, rib 11[12:14]) 5 times, M1, rib to end. 77[83:89] sts.
Change to larger needles and beg with a K row, work in St st until back measures 9[10¼:11]" from beg, ending with a P row.
Shape armholes
Bind off 4 sts at beg of next 2 rows.
Dec one st at each end of every row 5 times.
Dec one st at each end of every other row until 55[59:65] sts rem. **
Work even in St st until armhole measures 2½[2¾:3½]", ending with a P row.
Divide for opening
Next row K25[27:30], turn and leave rem sts on a st holder.
Cont in St st on these sts until armhole measures 5¼[5½:6¼]", ending with a P row.
Shape shoulder
Bind off at armhole edge on every other row 5[5:6] sts twice, 5[6:6] sts once and 10[11:12] sts once.
With RS facing, rejoin yarn to rem sts, bind off 5 center sts and complete to match first side, reversing shaping.

Front
Work as for back from ** to **.
Work even in St st until front measures 1½[1½:2]" less than back to shoulder shaping, ending with a P row.
Shape neck
Next row K21[22:25], turn and leave rem sts on a st holder. Keeping armhole edge even, dec one st at neck edge on every row 4 times, then one st on every other row until 15[16:18] sts rem. Work even until front measures same as back to shoulder.
Shape shoulder
Bind off at armhole edge on every other row 5[5:6] sts twice and 5[6:6] sts once.
Shape second side of neck
With RS facing rejoin yarn to rem sts, bind off 13[15:15] center sts loosely and complete to match first side reversing shaping.

Sleeves (make 2)
Using smaller needles, cast on 33[37:41] sts. Work in rib for 1½" as for back.
Inc row Rib 5, (M1, rib 8[9:10]) 3 times, M1, rib to end. 37[41:45] sts.
Change to larger needles and beg with a K row, work in St st, inc one st at each end of 5th[7th:7th] row and 6th[8th:8th] row 2[8:7] times. 43[59:61] sts.
1st and 3rd sizes
Inc one st at each end of 8th[10th] row twice. 55[65] sts.
All sizes
Work even until sleeve measures 11½[12¼:13¾]" from beg, ending with a P row.
Shape cap
Bind off 4 sts at beg of next 2 rows.
Dec one st at each end of next row and then every 4th row 6[5:5] times in all.

56

Dec one st at each end of next row and then every other row until 23 sts rem.
Bind off 3 sts at beg of next 4 rows.
Bind off rem 11 sts.

Buttonband

With RS of work facing and using smaller needles, pick up and K27 sts down right back opening.
1st row P2, * K1, P1, rep from * to last st, P1.
2nd row K2, * P1, K1, rep from * to last st, K1.

Rep last 2 rows once, then first row again.
Bind off loosely in rib.

Buttonhole band

With RS facing and using smaller needles, pick up and K27 sts down left back opening.
Work one row in rib as for buttonband.
Buttonhole row Rib 2, (bind off 2 sts, rib 8, including one st on needle after bind off) twice, bind off 2 sts, rib to end.

HELPING HAND

Making a twisted cord

Twisted cords are quick and easy to make. Here are the simple steps involved.

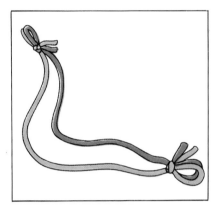

1 *Cut at least two pieces of yarn three times the length required for the finished cord. Knot the strands together at both ends, making loops as shown.*

2 *Slip one end onto a hook. Slip a pencil into the remaining end and turn it clockwise until the strands of yarn are twisted very tightly to the ends of the strands.*

3 *Remove the pencil and hold the cord tightly. Fold the cord in half at the center still keeping it taut and knot the two ends together.*

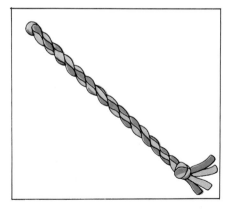

4 *Hold the knot and let go of the folded end. The strands will quickly twist together. Smooth down from the knotted end to even out the twists.*

Next row Rib to end, casting on 2 sts over those bound off.
Work 2 rows in rib. Bind off.

Neckband
Sew bands in position at lower edges. Join shoulder seams.
With RS facing and using set of double-pointed needles, pick up and K5 sts along buttonhole band, 9[11:13] sts across back neck to shoulder, 41[45:51] sts around front neck to left shoulder, 9[11:13] sts across right back neck and 5 sts along buttonband. 69[77:87] sts.
Work one row in rib as for buttonband.
Buttonhole row Rib 3, bind off 2 sts, rib to end.
Next row Rib to end, casting on 2 sts over those bound off in previous row.
Work 2 rows in rib.
Bind off loosely in rib.

To finish
Foll chart, draw appliqué pieces onto paper enlarging as indicated.
Then trace shapes onto remnants using fabric tracing paper.
Iron interfacing onto WS of fabric remnants.
Cut out shapes and baste in position on sweater. Using buttonhole and herringbone stitch, sew appliqué pieces (except fish) in position. (See page 79 for embroidery stitches.)
Cut ribbon to form mast, number seven on sail and collar on woman in boat. Baste, then sew in position.
Make a twisted cord with navy and white yarns for fishing rod (see Helping Hand). Sew fishing rod to sweater and sew tip of fish to end of it.
Embroider two seagulls in straight stitches, using navy yarn and foll photo.
Join side and sleeve seams. Set in sleeves, easing in fullness at cap.
Sew on buttons. Press seams lightly.
Sew lace around neck and armbands.

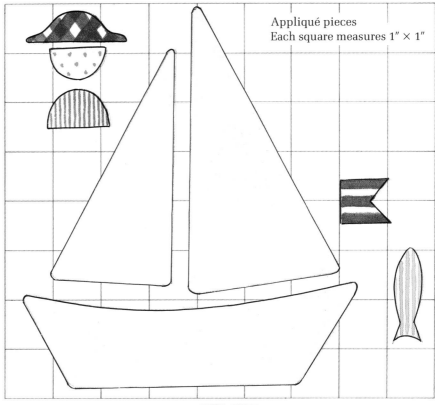

Appliqué pieces
Each square measures 1″ × 1″

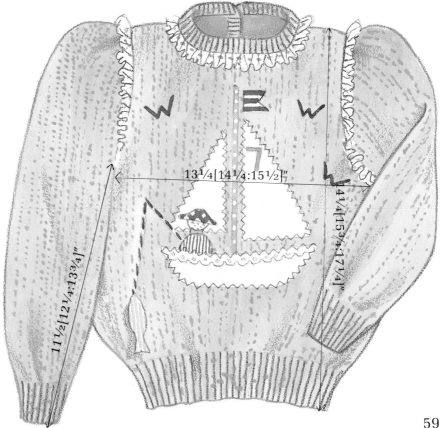

11½[12¼:13¾]″   13¼[14¼:15½]″   14¼[15¾:17¼]″

Ridged Vest

Knitting ridged patterns can be a creative delight! Here is your chance to play with color and make something original with purl ridges or garter stitch ridges.

Size
To fit 28" chest
Length 20½"

Materials
☐ 3½oz of a knitted worsted weight yarn in main color MC
☐ 1¾oz in each of 3 contrasting colors A, B and C
☐ One pair of size 6 knitting needles

Gauge
21 sts and 41 rows to 4" over purl ridges pat using size 6 needles.

To save time, take time to check gauge.

Back and fronts
Back and fronts are worked in one piece to armholes.
Using MC, cast on 132 sts. Beg with a K row, work 10 rows in St st.
Hem row *K next st and corresponding st of cast-on row tog, rep from * to end.
Work purl ridges pat (see page 61) for 12½" from hem, ending with a 5th row of pat.

Divide for armholes
Next row Keeping pat correct, work 17 sts in pat and leave on a st holder, bind off next 18 sts, work 62 sts in pat and leave on a st holder, bind-off next 18 sts, work 17 sts in pat.
Left front
Cont in pat on first 17 sts until armhole measures approx 8", ending with an 11th row of pat or

with a row in MC.
Bind off.

Back

With WS facing, rejoin yarn to 62 sts of back and cont to work in purl ridges pat until back measures same as left front to shoulder.
Bind off.

Right front

With WS facing, rejoin yarn to 17 sts of right front and cont to work in purl ridges pat until right front measures same as back and left front to shoulder.
Bind off.

Armbands

Join shoulder seams.
With RS facing and using MC, pick up and K84 sts around armhole.
Beg with a P row, work 10 rows in St st.
Bind off.
Join side and armband seams.
Turn armbands to WS and sew down.

Front band

With RS facing and using MC, pick up and K111 sts up right front, 28 sts across back neck and 111 sts down left front.
Beg with a P row, work 10 rows in St st.
Bind off.

To finish

Turn front band to WS and sew down.
Do not press.

VARIATIONS

Give in to your creative urge and try varying the yarns and colors on this simple vest. A smooth and a mohair yarn make an especially interesting texture contrast. Use the purl ridges as instructed in the pattern or the more classic garter stitch ridges.

Purl ridges

This pat is worked in a main color (MC) and 3 contrasting colors (A, B and C).
1st and 3rd rows (WS) With MC, P.
2nd row With MC, K.
4th, 5th, 7th and 9th rows With A, K.
6th, 8th and 10th rows With A, P.
11th row With A, *pick up st in 7th row below next st on left-hand needle and K it tog with next st, rep from * to end.
12th, 14th, 16th and 18th rows With MC, K.
13th, 15th and 17th rows With MC, P.
These 18 rows form pat and are rep throughout, changing to B, then C in turn on the 4th-11th rows.

Garter stitch ridges

This pat is worked in a main color (MC) and 3 contrasting colors (A, B and C).
1st, 3rd and 5th rows With MC, K.
2nd, 4th and 6th rows With MC, P.
7th and 8th rows With A, K.
These 8 rows form pat and are rep throughout, changing to B, then C in turn on 7th and 8th rows.

Space Sweater

They'll be off to the moon with the space invaders dressed in a super sparkly sweater! Worked in a fun colorwork pattern, this sweater has a smart crossover collar.

Sizes
To fit 28[30:32]″ chest
Length 15¾[17¾:19¾]″
Sleeve seam 11½[13:14½]″
Note Instructions for larger sizes are in brackets [ ]; where there is only one set of figures it applies to all sizes.

Materials
- ☐ 3[3:5]oz of a sport weight yarn in main color MC (black)
- ☐ 1½oz in each of 5 contrasting colors A (lilac), B (red), C (yellow), D (navy) and E (green)
- ☐ 1½[1½:2]oz in a lightweight metallic yarn F (silver)
- ☐ One pair each of sizes 3 and 6 knitting needles

Gauge
24 sts and 30 rows to 4″ over St st using size 6 needles.

To save time, take time to check gauge.

Note If necessary, use 2 strands of F tog throughout.

Back
*Using smaller needles and MC, cast on 84[90:96] sts. Work 16 rows K1, P1 rib.
Change to larger needles and beg with a K row, cont in St st, working color pat foll chart.
Work even until 56[66:76] rows have been worked from chart.
Shape armholes
Bind off 6 sts at beg of next 2 rows.
Dec one st at beg of every row until 66[70:72] sts rem.*
Work even for 38[38:36] more rows.

Shape shoulders
Bind off 16[17:18] sts at beg of next 2 rows.
Bind off rem 34[36:36] sts.

Front
Work as for back from * to *.
Divide for neck
Keeping pat correct, K33[35:36] sts, turn and sl rem sts onto a st holder. Complete left side of neck first.
Dec one st at beg of next row and then every other row until 16[17:18] sts rem.
Work even for 4[2:0] rows. Bind off.

With RS facing, rejoin yarn to sts on st holder.
Complete to match first side of neck, reversing shaping.

Sleeves (make 2)
Using smaller needles and MC, cast on 44[46:50] sts. Work 16 rows in K1, P1 rib.
Change to larger needles and beg with a K row, cont in St st, foll chart and beg with 55th row.
Work 2 rows.
Inc one st at each end of next row and then every 8th row until there are 60[66:72] sts.
Work even until 72[82:92] rows have been worked from chart.
Shape cap
Bind off 6 sts at beg of next 2 rows.

1st and 2nd sizes only
Dec one st at beg of next 2 rows.
Work 2 rows.
Rep last 4 rows 3[1] times more.
All sizes
Dec one st at beg of every row until 30 sts rem. Bind off.

Collar
Join left shoulder seam.
With RS facing and using smaller needles and MC, pick up and K34[36:36] sts across back neck, 32 sts down left side of front neck. 66[68:68] sts.
Work 30 rows in K1, P1 rib.
Bind off loosely in rib.
With RS facing and using smaller needles and MC, pick up and K32 sts up right side of front neck.

Work 30 rows in K1, P1 rib.
Bind off loosely in rib.

To finish
Press pieces lightly on WS with warm iron.
Join right shoulder seam.
Join collar seam.
Fold collar in half onto WS and sew in place. Cross ends of collar right over left at center front and sew down.
Join side and sleeve seams. Set in sleeves.

HELPING HAND

Stranding yarn
When using two colors or more, the yarn color not in use passes in loose strands across the back of the work behind the contrasting stitches until it is needed again. Be careful not to pull the color not in use too tightly on the wrong side of the work, which causes puckering.

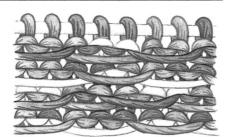

1 *Since only two colors are used per row it is possible to control one with each hand. If you are right-handed you will probably prefer to use this hand to control the most often-used color.*

2 *When the right-hand color is being used, the left hand holds the other color out of the way. When the left-hand color is being used, the right holds the other.*

3 *On purl rows hold the strands at the front of the work. The back of the work shows the stranded yarns over the purl stitches.*

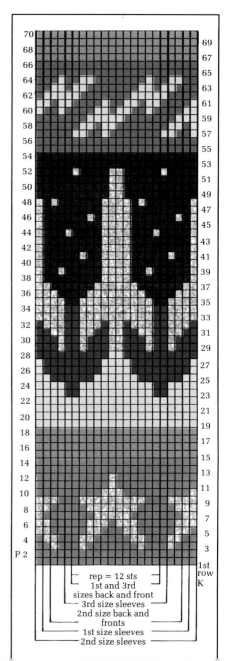

Quilted Jacket

The front and back sections of this stockinette stitch jacket with hood are lined and quilted. The top stitching is worked in a symmetrical zigzag pattern, using a contrasting color.

Sizes
To fit 20[22:24]″ chest
Length 14¼[15½:16½]″
Sleeve seam 11½[12¼:13]″
Note Instructions for larger sizes are in brackets [ ]; where there is only one set of figures it applies to all sizes.

Materials
☐ 9[9:11] oz of a fingering weight yarn
☐ One pair each of sizes 1 and 3 knitting needles
☐ ½ yd of 36″-wide fabric in contrasting or matching color for lining
☐ ½ yd of 36″-wide batting
☐ Strong cotton thread in a contrasting color

Gauge
30 sts and 41 rows to 4″ over St st using size 3 needles.

To save time, take time to check gauge.

Back
Using smaller needles, cast on 80[84:88] sts. Work in K2, P2 rib for 2″.
1st size Next row Rib 2, (pick up strand between st just worked and next st and work into back of it – called M1 –, rib 4) 19 times, M1, rib 2.
2nd and 3rd sizes Next row Rib 2, (M1, rib 5:4) 6 times, (M1, rib [4:5]) [6:8] times, (M1, rib [5:4]) 5 times, M1, rib [3:2]. 100[102:108] sts.
Change to larger needles and work in St st, beg with a K row, until back measures 8¼[9:9¾]″ from beg, ending with a WS row.
Shape armholes
Bind off 10[9:9] sts at beg of next 2 rows. 80[84:90] sts.
Work even in St st until back measures 13½[14½:15¾]″ from beg, ending with a WS row.
Shape neck
Next row K35[37:40] sts, turn and leave rem 45[47:50] sts on a st holder.
Work on these 35[36:39] sts only for first side of neck.
Bind off at neck edge on next and every other row 3[4:4] sts once, 3 sts once, 2[3:3] sts once and 2 sts once.
Bind off rem 25[25:28] sts.
Shape second side of neck
Sl 10 center sts onto a st holder and rejoin yarn to rem 35[37:40] sts.
Work on these sts for 2nd side of neck as for first side, reversing all shaping.

Left front
Using smaller needles, cast on 34[34:38] sts. Work in K2, P2 rib for 2″.

Next row Rib 2, (M1, rib 3) 4[2:5] times, (M1, rib 2) 4[10:2] times, (M1, rib 3) 4[2:5] times. 46[48:50] sts.
Change to larger needles and work in St st, beg with a K row, until front measures same as back to armhole, ending with a WS row.
Shape armhole
Bind off 10[9:9] sts at beg of next row. 36[39:41] sts.
Work even in St st until front measures 12¼[13½:14½]″ from beg.
Shape neck
Bind off at neck edge on next and every other row 3 sts twice and 2 sts 2[3:3] times.
Dec one st at beg of every other row until there are 25[25:28] sts.
Work even on these sts until front measures 14¼[15½:16½]″ from beg. Bind off.

Right front
Work as for left front, reversing all shaping.

Sleeves (make 2)
Using smaller needles, cast on 56[60:60] sts. Work in K2, P2 rib for 1½″.
Next row Rib 5, (M1, rib 9[10:5]) 5[5:11] times, M1, rib 6[5:2]. 62[66:72] sts.
Work in St st, inc one st at each end of every 5th[5th:6th] row until there are 94[100:106] sts.
Work even on these sts until sleeve measures 11½[12¼:13]″ from beg. Bind off.

Hood
** Using larger needles, cast on 48 sts.

1st and every other row P to end.
2nd row K to last 8 sts, turn.
4th row K to last 16 sts, turn.
6th row K to last 24 sts, turn.
8th row K to last 32 sts, turn.
10th row K to last 40 sts, turn.
12th row K to end. **
Cont on these sts in St st, inc one st at beg of every 12th row until there are 54 sts.
Cont on these sts in St st until hood measures 9″ from beg.
Shape hood
Dec one st at beg of every other row until 34 sts rem, then bind off 2 sts at beg of next 2 rows. 30 sts.
Hood should measure 13″ from beg.
Cont in St st and with WS facing, cast on 2 sts at each end of every other row twice, then inc one st at each end of every other row until there are 54 sts.
Hood should measure 17″ from beg.
With WS facing, dec one st at each end of every 12th row until 48 sts rem.
Work even on these sts until hood measures 24¾″ from beg.
Work from ** to **, working P rows in K and K rows in P.
Bind off.

To finish
Press front and back sections lightly. Pin front and back sections to the lining and cut out neatly allowing ⅝″ seam allowance. Do the same for the batting, omitting seam allowance. Pin, then baste the three sections tog, making sure the seam allowance is folded under the batting. Using strong cotton thread, work the diagonal zigzag lines over the pieces 1¼″ apart.
Join sleeve seams. Set in sleeves. Fold hood in half and stitch in place.

Front bands
Mark positions of 6 buttonholes along right front, the first ½″ from lower edge, the last at neck edge and the rest evenly spaced between. Using smaller needles, pick up and K91[95:99] sts up left front, 156 around hood, and 91[95:99] sts

down right front. 338[346:354] sts.
Work in K2, P2 rib for ¼″, then work buttonholes over next 2 rows by binding off 2 sts for each buttonhole in first row and casting on 2 sts in 2nd row. Cont in rib

until band measures ¾″ from beg.
Bind off in rib.
Sew on buttons to correspond with buttonholes.
Press seams lightly on WS with warm iron.

HELPING HAND

Quilted knitting
Although quilting is an embroidery technique, it can be used to add interest and texture to knitting. It is used for detailing shoulders, yokes, hems and pockets or even whole front and back sections.
The most popular form of quilting is wadded quilting. For this method, three layers of material are used; the top knitted fabric, the batting and lining fabric are sandwiched together and stitched through in a decorative pattern. The stitching can be worked in either a backstitch, running stitch or a chain stitch. It can be worked in a matching thread or a contrasting yarn depending on the finished effect required.

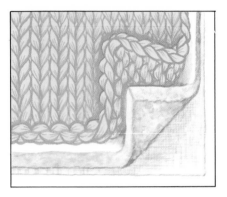

1 *Sandwich the three layers of fabric together on a flat surface. Smooth out any wrinkles. Be careful not to stretch the knitted fabric. The batting should measure the same as the knitted piece and the lining should have a ⅝″ seam allowance.*

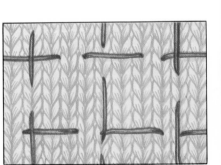

2 *Pin and baste through all three layers of fabric. Baste in horizontal and vertical rows about 1″ apart. This will prevent the layers shifting as they are quilted. As the edges are reached, when basting, turn the lining seam allowance under between the knitting and the batting.*

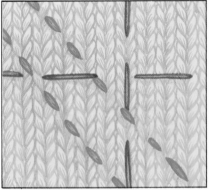

3 *Quilt in the desired pattern, using either a running stitch or a backstitch and working small stitches. Use the knitted stitches as a grid to help keep the pattern regular. Remove all the basting when the quilting is complete.*

Candy Vest

Candy spills from a make believe pocket on a simple-to-knit top. If trompe l'oeil motif does not suit your fancy, pick another and work it in your favorite colors.

Back
**Using smaller needles and A, cast on 84 sts. Work in K2, P2 rib for 2½".
Change to larger needles and MC.

Beg with a K row, work in St st until back measures 11" from beg, ending with a P row.
Shape armholes
Bind off 4 sts at beg of next 2 rows.

Size
To fit 28" chest
Length 16¼"

Materials
☐ 9oz of a sport weight yarn in main color MC
☐ 3½oz in contrasting color A
☐ Small amounts in 4 contrasting colors
☐ One pair each of size 3 and 6 knitting needles
☐ Tapestry needle

Gauge
22 sts and 31 rows to 4" over St st using size 6 needles.

To save time, take time to check gauge.

Candy Vest

Bind off 3 sts at beg of next 2 rows.
Bind off 2 sts at beg of next 2 rows.
Dec one st at beg of next 2 rows. 64
sts. **
Work even in St st until back
measures 16¼" from beg, ending
with a P row.

Shape shoulders
Bind off 5 sts at beg of next 6 rows.
Leave rem 34 sts on st holder for
back neck.

Front
Work as for back from ** to **
Work even in St st until front
measures 13¾", ending with a P
row.

Divide for neck
Next row K24, turn and leave rem
sts on a st holder.
Cont on these sts for first side of neck.
Dec one st at neck edge on next 9
rows.
Work even until front measures
same as back to shoulder shaping,
ending at armhole edge.

Shape shoulder
Bind off at armhole edge on every
other row 5 sts 3 times.
With RS facing, sl center 16 sts
onto st holder.
Rejoin yarn to rem sts on st holder.
Complete to match first side,
reversing shaping.

Neckband
Join one shoulder seam.
With RS facing and using smaller
needles and A, pick up and K80 sts
around neck.
Work in K2, P2 rib for 9 rows.
Bind off loosely in rib.

Armbands
Join other shoulder seam.
With RS facing and using smaller
needles and A, pick up and K90 sts
around armhole.
Work in K2, P2 rib for 9 rows.
Bind off in rib.

To finish
Join side seams. Work motif on
front using duplicate st. Press
lightly on WS with warm iron.

VARIATIONS
Work the candy and pocket
motif in duplicate stitch on the
front of the vest or choose one of
the other trompe l'oeil effects.
To enhance these convincing
details use a shiny yarn for the
embroidery to contrast with the
matt wool background.

Buttons

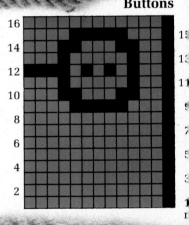

Pocketful of candy

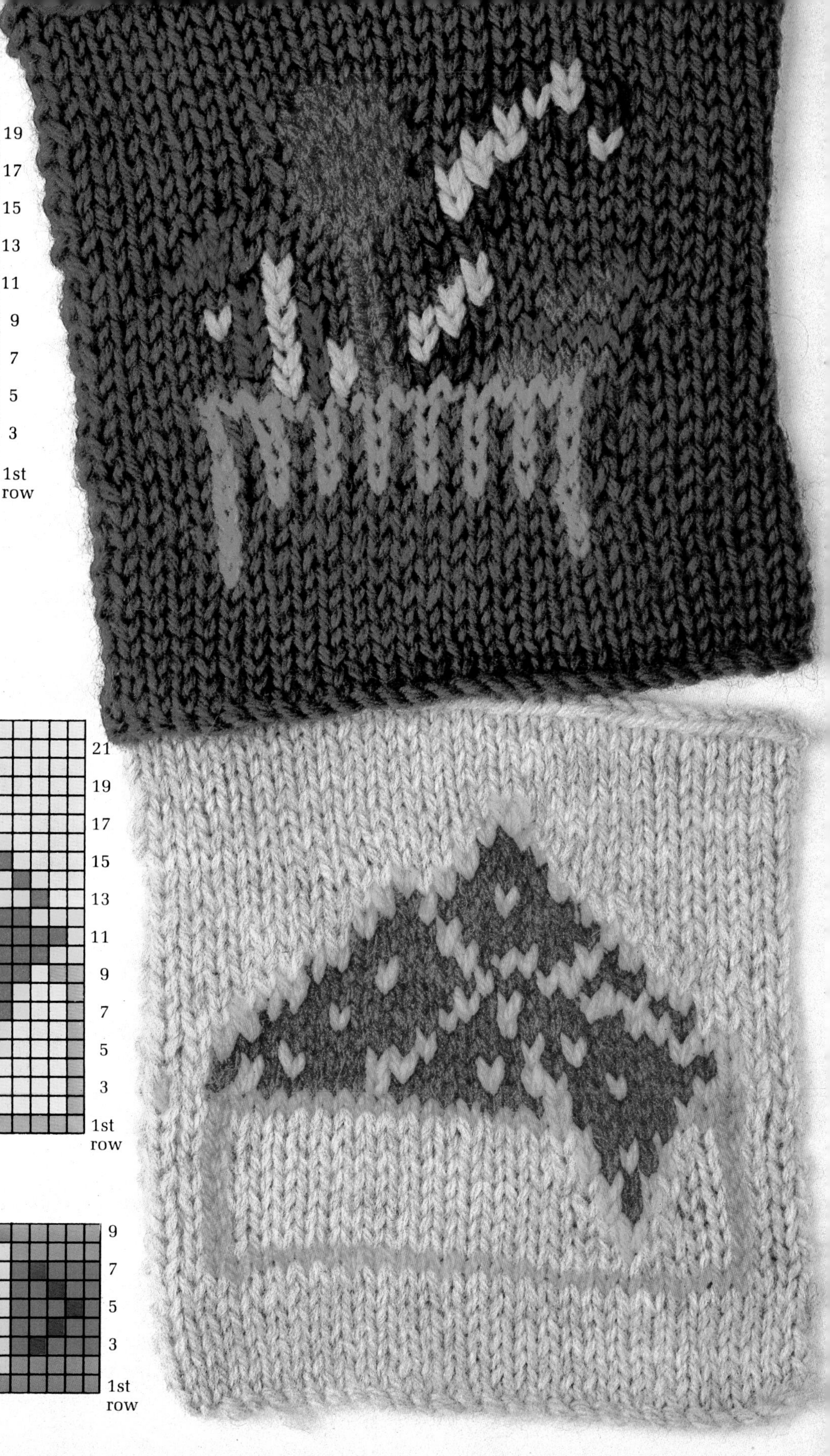

19
17
15
13
11
9
7
5
3
1st
row

Pocket-handkerchief

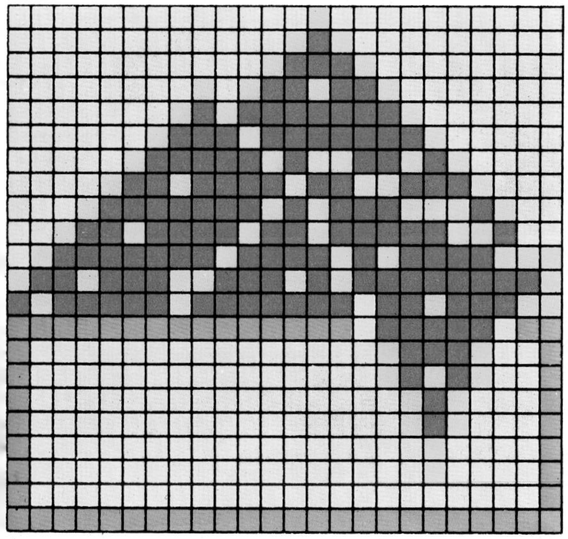

21
19
17
15
13
11
9
7
5
3
1st
row

Belt

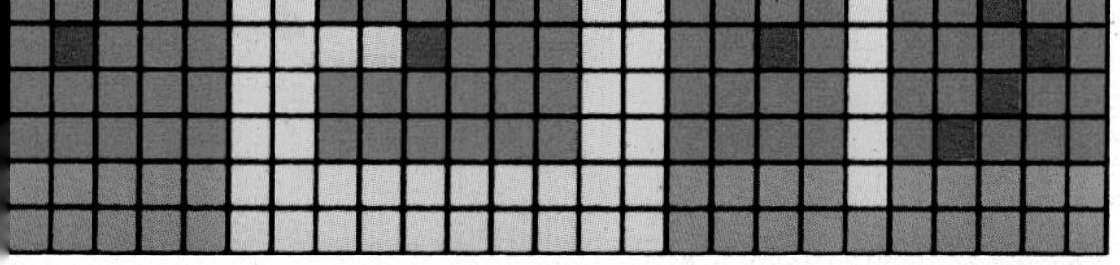

9
7
5
3
1st
row

Bouclé Jacket

This warm and woolly jacket is worked in a variegated bouclé with a smooth yarn for the yoke. You could get the same effect by working in stripes of subtle shades of a novelty yarn.

Sizes
To fit 25[26:28:30]″ chest
Length 19½[20¾:22:23¼]″
Sleeve seam 11[11½:11¾:12¼]″
Note Instructions for larger sizes are in brackets [ ]; where there is only one set of figures it applies to all sizes.

Materials
☐ 18[20:20:21]oz of a medium weight bouclé yarn A
☐ 3½[3½:6:6]oz of a bulky weight yarn B
☐ One pair each of sizes 5 and 7 knitting needles
☐ Size 9 circular knitting needle

Gauge
15 sts and 24 rows to 4″ over St st using size 7 needles and A.
14 sts and 18 rows to 4″ over St st using size 9 needles and B.

To save time, take time to check gauge.

Back
Using size 5 needles and A, cast on 56[58:62:66] sts. Work in K1, P1 rib for 1¼″.
Change to size 7 needles and beg with a K row, cont in St st until back measures 13[13½:13¾:14½]″ from beg, ending with a P row.
Shape raglan armholes
Dec one st at each end of next row and then every 4th row 1[2:2:2] times.
Dec one st at each end of every other row until 48 sts rem, ending with a P row.
Transfer these sts and leave on a st holder.

Left front
**Using size 5 needles and A, cast on 28[30:32:34] sts. Work in K1, P1 rib for 1¼″.
Change to size 7 needles and beg with a K row, cont in St st until front measures same as back to armhole shaping, ending with a P row.
Shape raglan armhole
Dec one st at armhole edge of next row. Work 3 rows.
Dec one st at armhole edge of next row and then every other row 0[2:4:6] times. 26 sts. **
Shape neck
Next row P8, leave these sts on a safety pin, P18.

Next row K2 tog, K16.
Next row P6, leave these sts on a safety pin, P11.
Next row K2 tog, K9.
Next row P10. Leave these sts on a safety pin.

Right front
Work as for left front from ** to **.
Work one row.
Shape neck
Next row K8, leave these sts on a safety pin, K16, K2 tog.
Next row P17.
Next row K6, leave these sts on a safety pin, K9, K2 tog.
Next row P10.
Leave these sts on a safety pin.

Sleeves (make 2)
Using size 5 needles and A, cast on 28[30:32:34] sts. Work in K1, P1 rib for 1¼".
Change to size 7 needles and beg with a K row, cont in St st, inc one st at each end of every 6th [6th:6th :5th] row until there are 44[48:52 :56] sts.
Work even until sleeve measures 11[11½:11¾:12¼]" from beg, ending with a P row.
Shape raglan top
Dec one st at each end of next row and then every other row until 34 sts rem, ending with a P row.
Leave these sts on a spare needle.

Yoke
With RS facing and using size 9 circular needle and B, K across 24 sts on safety pins on right front, K34 sts from right sleeve top, 48 sts on back neck, 34 sts on left sleeve top and K across 24 sts on safety pins on left front. 164 sts.
Work back and forth in rows as foll:
Next row P to end.
Next row K2, *K3, K2 tog, K3, rep from * to last 2 sts, K2. 144 sts.
Beg with a P row, work 3 rows in St st.
Next row K2, *K3, K2 tog, K2, rep from * to last 2 sts, K2. 124 sts.
Beg with a P row, work 3 rows in St st.

Next row K2, *K2, K2 tog, K2, rep from * to last 2 sts, K2. 104 sts.
Beg with a P row, work 3 rows in St st.
Next row K2, *K2, K2 tog, K1, rep from * to last 2 sts, K2. 84 sts.
Beg with a P row, work 3 rows in St st.
Next row K2, *K1, K2 tog, K1, rep from * to last 2 sts, K2. 64 sts.
Beg with a P row, work 3 rows in St st.
Next row K2, *K1, K2 tog, rep from * to last 2 sts, K2. 44 sts.
Next row P to end.
Leave these sts on a st holder.

Left front band
With RS of yoke sts facing and using size 5 needles and A, join in yarn to center of sts, K these 22 sts, pick up and K one st from corner of front neck (mark this st with a colored thread), pick up and K80 [82:84:86] sts down left front edge. 103[105:107:109] sts.
1st row (WS) (P1, K1) 40 [41:42:43] times, pick up strand between st just worked and next st and purl into back of it – called M1–, P1, M1, (K1, P1) 11 times.
2nd row (K1, P1) 11 times, K3, (P1, K1) 40 [41:42:43] times.
Cont in K1, P1 rib in this way, inc and working into St st one st at each side of marked st, until band measures 1¼"
Bind off in rib over ribbed section.

Right front band
With RS facing and using size 5 needles and A, pick up and K80[82:84:86] sts up right front edge, pick up and K one st from corner of front neck (mark this st with a colored thread), K across rem 22 sts on yoke. 103[105:107: 109] sts.
Complete to match left front band.

To finish
Join side and sleeve seams.
Do not press.

HELPING HAND
Holding stitches

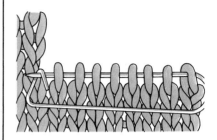

There are several ways of holding stitches which are to be worked into later. You can use purchased stitch holders, spare knitting needles, safety pins or even yarn in a contrasting color.
Stitch holders come in various sizes and are handy to have in your knitting basket.

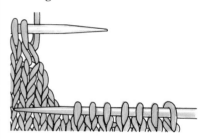

If you do not have a st holder to hand use a spare needle to hold stitches, but make sure it is not larger than the needles you are knitting with or it will stretch the stitches.

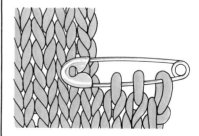

Small numbers of stitches can be left on safety pins. Place the stitches on the pin with the point facing the direction in which they are to be picked up again.

Loop Stitch Sweater

Knit a loop stitch sweater in bright buttery yellow with fresh white contrast. This one has an attractive stepped collar and two matching patch pockets on the front.

Sizes
To fit 26[28:30]″ chest
Length 20¾″
Sleeve seam 18¾″
Note Instructions for larger sizes are in brackets [ ]; where there is only one set of figures it applies to all sizes.

Materials
☐ 7[8:9]oz of a sport weight yarn in main color MC
☐ 7[8:9]oz in contrasting color A
☐ One pair each of sizes 3 and 4 knitting needles
☐ Cable needle

Gauge
36 sts and 38 rows to 4″ over loop st pat using size 4 needles.

To save time, take time to check gauge.

Back
**Using smaller needles and MC, cast on 116[126:136] sts. Work in K1, P1 rib for 39 rows.
Next row P9[14:8], pick up strand between st just worked and next st and work into back of it – called M1–, *P9[9:11], M1, rep from * to last 8[13:7] sts, P8[13:7]. 128 [138:148] sts.

Change to larger needles and beg loop st pat as foll:
1st and 3rd rows With A, K1, sl 1, *K4, sl 1, rep from * to last st, K1.
2nd and 4th rows P1, sl 1, *P4, sl 1, rep from * to last st, P1.
3rd-4th rows Rep first-2nd rows once.
5th row With MC, K1, *sl next 5 sts onto cable needle and hold at back

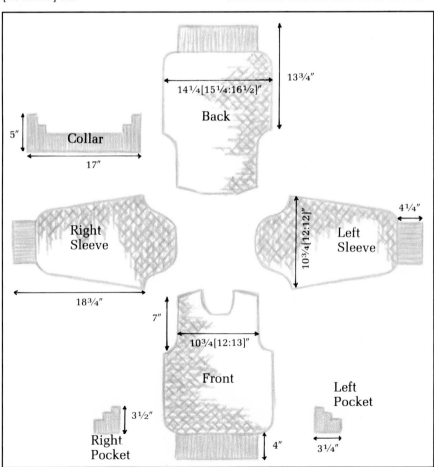

Collar 5″ 17″

Back 13¾″ 14¼[15¼:16½]″

Right Sleeve 18¾″

Left Sleeve 10¾[12:12]″ 4¼″

Front 7″ 10¾[12:13]″

Right Pocket 3½″

Left Pocket 4″ 3¼″

of work, K1, sl last 4 sts from cable needle onto left-hand needle, bring rem st on cable needle to front of work, K4, then K1 from cable needle – called cross 2 over 4 –, K4, rep from * ending last rep K1.

6th row With MC, K to end.

7th-10th rows Rep first-2nd rows twice.

11th row With MC, K6, *cross 2 over 4, K4, rep from * to last 2 sts, K2.

12th row With MC, K to end. These 12 rows form pat. Rep these 12 rows 7 times more.

Shape armholes

1st row With A, bind off 7 sts, K4 (including st used in binding off), *sl 1, K4, rep from * to last 2 sts, K2.

2nd row Bind off 7 sts, P4 (including st used in binding off), * sl 1, P4, rep from * to end.

3rd row K2 tog, K2, *sl 1, K4, rep from * to last 5 sts, sl 1, K2, K2 tog.

4th row P2 tog, P1, *sl 1, P4, rep from * to last 4 sts, sl 1, P1, P2 tog.

5th row With MC, K2 tog, *cross 2 over 4, K4, rep from * to last 8 sts, cross 2 over 4, K2 tog.

6th row With MC, K2 tog, K to last 2 sts, K2 tog.

7th row With A, K2 tog, K3, *sl 1, K4, rep from * to last 6 sts, sl 1, K3, K2 tog.

8th row P2 tog, P2, *sl 1, P4, rep from * to last 5 sts, sl 1, P2, P2 tog.

9th row K2 tog, K1, *sl 1, K4, rep from * to last 4 sts, sl 1, K1, K2 tog.

10th row P2 tog, *sl 1, P4, rep from * to last 3 sts, sl 1, P2 tog. 98[108: 118] sts. **

Work even, working 11th-12th pat rows once, then 1st-12th pat rows 5 times and 1st-6th rows once more.

Shape shoulders

Bind off 8[9:10] sts at beg of next 8 rows. Leave the rem 34[36:38] sts on a st holder.

Front

Work as for back from ** to **. Work even, working 11th-12th pat rows once, then first-12th pat rows twice.

Divide for neck

1st row With A, K1, (sl 1, K4) 7[8:9] times, K1, turn and leave rem 61 [66:71] sts on a st holder. Complete left side of neck first.

2nd row P2 tog, P3, (sl 1, P4) 6[7:8] times, sl 1, P1.

3rd row K1, (sl 1, K4) 6[7:8] times, sl 1, K2, K2 tog.

4th row P2 tog, P1, (sl 1, P4) 6[7:8] times, sl 1, P1.

5th row With MC, K1, (cross 2 over 4) 3[3:4] times, K1[6:1], K2 tog. 33[38:43] sts.

6th row With MC, K to end. Work even until front measures same as back to shoulder shaping, ending at armhole edge.

Loop Stitch Sweater

Shape shoulder
Bind off at armhole edge on every other row 8[9:10] sts 3 times and 9[11:13] sts once.
Return to sts on st holder, sl the center 24 sts onto another st holder and join in yarn to neck edge.
1st row With A, K1, (K4, sl 1) 7 [8:9] times, K1.
2nd row P1, (sl 1, P4) 6[7:8] times, sl 1, P3, P2 tog.
3rd row K2 tog, K2, (sl 1, K4) 6[7:8] times, sl 1, K1.
4th row P1, (sl 1, P4) 6[7:8] times, sl 1, P1, P2 tog.
5th row With MC, K2 tog, sl 1, (K4, cross 2 over 4) 3[3:4] times, K1 [6:1]. 33[38:43] sts.
6th row With MC, K to end.
Complete to match first side of neck, reversing shaping.

Sleeves (make 2)
Using smaller needles and MC, cast on 58[68:68] sts. Work in K1, P1 rib for 40 rows.
Change to larger needles and work 1st-12th pat rows as for back.
Cont in pat, inc one st at each end of next row and then every 6th row until there are 98[108:108] sts.
Work even until sleeve measures approx 18¾" from beg, ending with a WS row.
Shape cap
Work first-4th [first-10th:first-10th] rows of armhole shaping as for back.
Keeping pat correct, dec one st at each end of next row and then every other row until 30 [34:34] sts rem.
Bind off.

Collar
Using smaller needles and MC, cast on 171 sts. Work in rib as foll:
1st row Sl 1 purlwise, *K1, P1, rep from * to end.
2nd row Sl 1 knitwise, *P1, K1, rep from * to end.
Rep last 2 rows 10 times more.
Next row Sl 1 purlwise, rib 26, leave these sts on a st holder, bind off 117, rib 27.

Work first collar point. Rib 9 rows.
Next row Bind off 12, rib to end.
Rib 9 rows. Bind off in rib.
Rejoin yarn to sts on st holder.
Rib 10 rows.
Next row Bind off 12, rib to end.
Rib 9 rows.
Bind off in rib.

Pockets (make 2)
Using smaller needles and MC, cast on 33 sts. Work 13 rows in rib as for collar.
Next row Bind off 10 sts, rib to end.

Rib 9 rows.
Next row Bind off 10 sts, rib to end.
Rib 9 rows.
Bind off in rib.

To finish
Join shoulder, side and sleeve seams.
Set in sleeves.
Position pockets on front and sew in place.
Sew on collar. Fold back cuffs.
Press seams lightly on WS with warm iron.

HELPING HAND

Crossing two over four
Many original stitch patterns can be created by elongating stitches and then crossing or twisting the loops to form raised diagonal lines on the surface of the background stitch.

1 *This technique is used on the 5th and 11th pattern rows in the sweater instructions. Slip the next five stitches onto a cable needle and hold it at the back of the work. Knit one stitch from the left-hand needle as usual.*

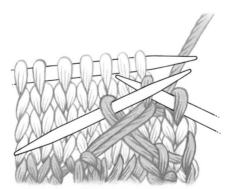

2 *Slip the last four stitches from the cable needle back onto the left-hand needle. Bring the remaining stitch on the cable needle to the front of the work.*

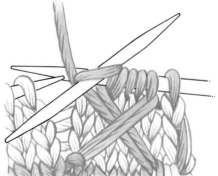

3 *Knit four from the left-hand needle, then knit the stitch on the cable needle.*

VARIATIONS

These loop stitches are worked in the same type of technique as the loop stitch pattern in the sweater instructions, but create very different effects and textures. In order to adapt the sweater instructions to these variations add 3 extra stitches when increasing across the ribbing on back and sleeves.

Cross-stitched stripe

This stitch works over a multiple of 10 stitches, plus 1 extra and uses three colors (A, B, C).

1st row (WS) With A, P to end.
2nd row With A, K to end.
3rd row With A, P6, *P1 winding yarn twice around needle, P2, P1 winding yarn twice around needle, P6, rep from *, ending last rep P1.
4th row With B, K1, *sl 1 allowing extra loop to fall, K2, sl 1 allowing extra loop to fall, K6, rep from * to end.
5th row With B, K6, *yarn to front of work, sl 1 purlwise, yarn to back of work – called sl 1 with yarn in front (wyif) –, K2, sl 1 wyif, K6, rep from *, ending last rep K1.
6th row With B, K1, * sl 1 purlwise, K2, sl 1 purlwise, K6, rep from * to end.
7th-9th rows Rep 5th-6th rows once, then 5th row again.
10th row With A, K1, * sl next st off left-hand needle and hold at front of work, K 3rd st on left-hand needle, then first, then 2nd st and discard all sts at the same time, return sl st onto left-hand needle and K – called cross 4 –, K6, rep from * to end.
11th row With A, P to end.
12th row With A, K to end.
13th row With A, P1, *P1 winding yarn twice around needle, P2, P1 winding yarn twice around needle, P6, rep from * to end.
14th row With C, K6, *sl 1 allowing extra loop to fall, K2, sl 1 allowing extra loop to fall, K6, rep from * ending last rep K1.
15th row With C, K1, *sl 1 wyif, K2, sl 1 wyif, K6, rep from * to end.
16th row With C, K6, *sl 1 purlwise, K2, sl 1 purlwise, K6, rep from *, ending last rep K1.
17th-19th rows Rep 15th-16th rows once, then 15th row again.
20th row With A, K6, *cross 4, K6, rep from *, ending last rep K1.
These 20 rows form pat and are rep throughout.

Popcorn loop stitch

This stitch works over a multiple of 5 stitches, plus 1 extra and uses four colors (A, B, C, D).

1st row (WS) With A, P to end.
2nd row K to end.
3rd row P1, *P1 winding yarn twice around needle, P2, P1 winding yarn twice around needle, P1, rep from * to end.
4th row With B, K1, sl 1 allowing extra loop to fall, K2, sl 1 allowing extra loop to fall, (K1, yo, K1, yo, K1) all into next st, rep from *, ending last rep K1.
5th row With B, K1, *yarn to front of work – called yft –, sl 1, P2, sl 1, yarn to back of work – called ybk –, K5, rep from * to last 5 sts, sl 1, P2, sl 1, ybk, K1.
6th row With B, K1 * ybk, sl 1, K2, sl 1, P5, rep from * to last 5 sts, ybk, sl 1, K2, sl 1, K1.
7th row With B, K1, *yft, sl 1, P2, sl 1, K2 tog, K3 tog, pass the 2nd st on right-hand needle over the last st, rep from * to last 5 sts, yft, sl 1, P2, sl 1, ybk, K1.
8th row With A, K1, * sl next st off left-hand needle and hold at front of work, sl 2, sl next st off needle and hold at front of work, return first st held back onto left-hand needle, sl 2 sts on right-hand needle back onto left-hand needle, return 2nd st held back onto left-hand needle, K5, rep from * to end.
These 8 rows form pat and are rep throughout, changing to C, then D in turn for 4th-7th rows.

Kangaroo Sweater

This witty sweater will put a smile on anyone's face! The kangaroo and sun are knit in and the appliqué and embroidered details are added later.

Sizes
To fit 24[26:28]″ chest
Length 14[15½:16½]″
Sleeve seam 9¾[11½:13]″
Note Instructions for larger sizes are in brackets [ ]; where there is only one set of figures it applies to all sizes.

Materials
☐ 3½[3½:6]oz of a sport weight yarn in main color MC (blue)
☐ 1¾[1¾:3½]oz in contrasting color A (yellow)
☐ 1oz in contrasting color B (pink)
☐ Small amounts of red and green
☐ One pair each of sizes 3 and 6 knitting needles
☐ Remnants of fabric and ribbon for appliqué
☐ Dark pink sewing thread
☐ Tapestry needle
☐ Small stuffed animal for pouch

Gauge
22 sts and 30 rows to 4″ over St st using size 6 needles.

To save time, take time to check gauge.

Note When working kangaroo, use a separate ball for each block of color instead of stranding across back of kangaroo. When changing colors, twist yarns to avoid holes.

Back
* Using smaller needles and A, cast on 64[70:76] sts. Work in K1, P1 rib for 2″.
Next row Rib 4[8:6], (pick up strand between st just worked and next st and work into back of it – called M1 –, rib 6[6:7]) 10 times, rib 0[2:0]. 74[80:86] sts. *
Change to larger needles and beg with a K row, work 32 rows in St st. Break off A and join in MC.
Beg with a K row, work 18[26:34] rows in St st in MC.
Shape armholes
**Cont working in MC and bind off 5 sts at beg of next 2 rows.
Dec one st at each end of next row and then every other row 4 times. 54[60:66] sts. **
Work 29[31:33] more rows in St st.
Shape shoulders
Bind off 6[6:7] sts at beg of next 4 rows.
Bind off 5[7:7] sts at beg of next 2 rows. Leave rem 20[22:24] sts on a st holder for back neck.

Pouch lining
Using larger needles and B, cast on 10 sts and work 12 rows in St st. Leave sts on a st holder.

Front
Work as for back from * to *.
Change to larger needles and beg with a K row, work 3 rows in St st.
Beg pat from chart as foll:

4th row P32[35:38] A, 7 B, 35[38:41] A.
5th row K36[39:42] A, K7 B, K31[34:37] A.
These rows set the position of the pat given in the chart. Work 6th to 28th rows foll chart.
Place pocket
Next row K27[30:33], sl next 10 sts onto a safety pin, K across 10 sts from pouch, K37[40:43].
Work 30th to 50th[58th:66th] rows foll chart.
Cont in pat foll chart, work as for back from ** to **, then work 23[25:25] more rows.
Shape neck
Cont in pat as set, K21[23:25], K2 tog, turn and work on these sts only.
Dec one st at neck edge on next 5 rows. 17[19:21] sts.
Work 0[2:2] rows in st st.

76

Shape shoulder
Bind off at armhole edge on every other row 6[6:7] sts twice.
P one row.
Bind off 5[7:7] sts.
Second side of neck
With RS facing, sl center 8[10:12] sts onto a safety pin, rejoin yarn to rem 23[25:27] sts, K2 tog, K to end. Complete as for first side of neck, reversing shaping.

Sleeves (make 2)
Using smaller needles and A, cast on 36[38:40] sts. Work in K1, P1 rib for 2".
Next row Rib 4[5:6], (M1, rib 9) 3 times, M1, rib to end. 40[42:44] sts. Change to larger needles.
Break off A and join in MC. Beg with a K row, work in St st, inc one st each end of 3rd row and then every 8th row until there are 54[58:62] sts.
Cont working in St st until sleeve measures 9¾[11½:13]" from beg, ending with a WS row.
Shape cap
Bind off 5 sts at beg of next 2 rows.
Dec one st at each end of next row

14[15½:16½]"

13½[14½:15¾]"

9¾[11½:13]"

and then every other row 8[8:9:10] times.
P one row.
Bind off 3 sts at beg of next 8 rows.
Bind off rem 2[4:6] sts.

Neckband
Join right shoulder seam.
With RS facing and using smaller needles and MC, pick up and K12[13:14] sts down left side of neck, K across center 8[10:12] sts, pick up and K12[13:14] sts up right side of neck, then K across 20[22:24] sts of back neck inc 6 sts evenly. 58[64:70] sts.
Work 6 rows in K1, P1 rib.
Bind off loosely in rib.

Pouch top
Rejoin B to 10 sts left on safety pin. Using smaller needles, work 2 rows in K1, P1 rib. Bind off loosely in rib.

HELPING HAND

Stem stitch
Stem stitch is more decorative than back stitch and is particularly well suited to modelling curved outlines in embroidery. Stem stitch gives a thicker outline than back stitch, as the stitches actually overlap each other. If the stitches worked are short, stem stitch will give a well-defined ridge; if the stitches are longer, you can achieve a slightly feathery look. Stem stitch is worked from left to right, with the needle pointing from right to left along the stitching line.

Lazy daisy stitch
Lazy daisy stitch is a form of detached chain stitches. Several chain stitches are worked from a common center. Leaf sprays can be worked with three chain stitches and flowers with five or six.
Thread a blunt-ended needle with the contrasting color. Secure one end firmly at the back of the work. Bring the needle to the right side. This is now the center of the flower. Insert the needle again through the center and out a short distance away without pulling the needle through. Wrap the yarn around the needle loosely and pull the needle through. Secure the loop with neat stitch. One petal or leaf is now complete.

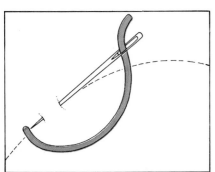

1 Bring the needle up on the right side of the fabric. Make a stitch to the right, bringing the point of the needle up part-way along the stitching line.

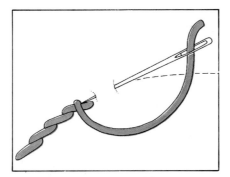

2 Make the next stitch in the same way so that the stitching follows a smooth line.

To finish

Join left shoulder seam. Join side and sleeve seams and set in sleeves. Sew pouch lining in place. Using remnants of washable fabric, cut out a hat and sunshade adding a ¼" hem allowance. Turn under ¼" hems and baste. Make a ruffle using ribbon and sew to lower edge of hat.

Sew hat and sunshade to sweater front with small stitches. Using dark pink thread, embroider ribs on sunshade and arm and leg on kangaroo in stem st (see Helping Hand). Using red yarn, embroider eyes on sun and mouth and nose on kangaroo in short sts, mouth on sun in stem st, sunshade handle in chain st (see page 163), sunshade

trim in zigzag straight sts, tip of sunshade and flowers in lazy daisy st (see Helping Hand). Embroider sun rays in duplicate st (see page 50) and stem st as indicated on chart, using A. Using green, embroider eye on kangaroo in short st and stems and leaves in lazy daisy st. Press seams lightly on WS with warm iron.

Artist's Vest

Trim the pockets of this colorful vest with pockets with mitered borders. Finish off the masterpiece with bright colored fun buttons – a detail any artist would relish.

Sizes
To fit 24[26:28:30]" chest
Length 14[15¾:17¼:19]"
Note Instructions for larger sizes are in brackets [ ]; where there is only one set of figures it applies to all sizes.

Materials
- ☐ 6[6:6:7] oz of a sport weight yarn in main color MC (blue)
- ☐ 1¾ oz in each of 3 contrasting colors A (red), B (yellow) and C (green)
- ☐ One pair each of sizes 3 and 6 knitting needles
- ☐ 5 buttons

Gauge
24 sts and 32 rows to 4" over St st using size 6 needles.

___

To save time, take time to check gauge.

___

Back
Using smaller needles and MC, cast on 73[79:85:91] sts. Work in rib as foll:
1st row (RS) K1, * P1, K1, rep from * to end.
2nd row P1, * K1, P1, rep from * to end.
Rep last 2 rows for 2", ending with a first row.
Inc row Rib 6, * pick up strand between st just worked and next st and work into back of it – called M1 –, rib 10[11:12:13], rep from * 5 times, M1, rib to end. 80[86:92:98] sts.
Change to larger needles and beg with a K row, work in St st until back measures 9[10¼:11:12¼]", ending with a P row.
Shape armholes
Bind off 4 sts at beg of next 2 rows.
Dec one st at each end of next 5 rows.
Dec one st at each end of every other row until 58[62:68:72] sts rem.
Work even in St st until armhole measures 5[5½:6¼:6¾]", ending with a P row.
Shape shoulders
Bind off 5[6:6:7] sts at beg of next 4 rows.
Bind off 6[5:7:6] sts at beg of next 2 rows.
Bind off rem 26[28:30:32] sts.

Left front
Using smaller needles, cast on 37[39:43:45] sts. Work in rib as for back.
Inc row Rib 6[4:8:6], * M1, rib 12[10:14:11], rep from * 1[2:1:2] times more, M1, rib to end. 40[43:

46:49] sts.
Change to larger needles and beg with a K row, work in St st until front measures same as back to armhole shaping, ending with a P row.
Shape armhole and front slope
Next row Bind off 4 sts, K to end.
Next row P to end.
Next row K2 tog, K to last 4 sts, K2 tog, K2.
Next row P to last 2 sts, P2 tog.
Rep last 2 rows once more, then first row again.
Next row P to end.
Next row K2 tog, K to last 4 sts, K2 tog, K2.
Rep last 2 rows until 24[25:28:29] sts rem.
P one row.
Keeping armhole edge even, cont to dec one st at center front slope as before on next and foll 4th[3rd:1st:2nd] rows, then one st on every 4th row until 16[17:19:20] sts rem.
Work even until front measures same as back to shoulder shaping, ending with a P row.
Shape shoulder
Bind off at armhole edge on every other row 5[6:6:7] sts twice.
Work one row. Bind off rem sts.

Right front
Work as for left front, reversing shaping and noting that K2 tog tbl will be worked in place of K2 tog at center front slope shaping.

Left pocket
Using larger needles and MC, cast on 17 sts. Beg with a K row, work 2 rows in MC, then work 18 rows of St st in stripe pat as foll:

2 rows MC, 2 rows A, 2 rows MC,
2 rows B, 2 rows MC, 2 rows C.
Rep from * to * once.
Next row Using C, K to end.
Change to smaller needles and
work in rib as foll:
1st row P1, * K1, P1, rep from * to
end.
2nd row K1, * P1, K1, rep from * to
end.
3rd row As first row.
Bind off loosely in rib.

Left pocket border
Using larger needles and C, cast on
55 sts.
1st row P18, mark next st, P17,
mark next st, P18.
Foll instructions for mitered corner
for 3 rows. Bind off evenly purlwise.
Sew in position neatly around
pocket aligning the edges.

Right pocket
Work in multi-colored stripes as for

left pocket, working the contrasting
rib in B.

Right pocket border
Work as for left pocket border,
using B.

Breast pocket
Using larger needles and MC, cast
on 13 sts.
Beg with a K row, work 2 rows in
MC, then work 14 rows of St st in

stripe pat as foll:
2 rows MC, 2 rows A, 2 rows MC, 2
rows B, 2 rows MC, 2 rows C, 2
rows MC.
Next row Using A, K to end.
Change to smaller needles and
work in rib as for left pocket
border.

Breast pocket border
Using larger needles and A, cast on
43 sts.
1st row P14, mark next st, P13,
mark next st, P14.
Complete as for left pocket border.

Girl's buttonhole band
** With RS facing and using
smaller needles and MC, beg at
lower right front edge and pick up
and K 60[68:74:82] sts to front
slope shaping, 39[43:45:47] sts to
shoulder and 13[13:15:15] sts to
center back neck. 112[124:134:144]
sts.
1st row P1, * K1, P1, rep from
* to end.
2nd row K1, * P1, K1, rep from *
to end.
3rd row As first row.
4th row Using B, rib 3, (bind off 2
sts, rib 11[13:15:17], including one
st on needle after bind-off) 4 times,
bind off 2 sts, rib to end.

5th row Using B, rib to end, casting
on 2 sts over those bound off.
6th row Using MC, as 2nd row.
7th row Using MC, as first row.
Bind off loosely in rib.

Girl's button band
** With RS facing and using
smaller needles and MC, beg at
center back neck and pick up and
K13[13:15:15] sts to left shoulder,
39[43:45:47] sts to beg of front
slope shaping and 60[68:74:82] sts
to lower front edge. 112[124:134
:144] sts. **
Work in rib as for buttonhole band,
omitting buttonholes.
Join bands at center back neck.

Boy's buttonhole band
Work as for girl's version button
band from ** to **.
1st row P1, * K1, P1, rep from * to
end.
2nd row K1, * P1, K1, rep from * to
end.
3rd row As first row.
4th row Using B, rib to last
60[68:74:82] sts, (bind off 2 sts, rib
11[13:15:17], including one st on
needle after bind off) 4 times, bind
off 2 sts, rib to end.
5th row Using B, rib to end, casting
on 2 sts over those bound off.

Change to MC and work 2 rows in
rib.
Bind off loosely in rib.

Boy's button band
Work as for girl's version
buttonhole band from ** to **.
Work in rib as for buttonhole band,
omitting buttonholes.
Join bands at center back neck.

Armbands
With RS facing and using smaller
needles and MC, pick up and
K69[75:85:91] sts evenly around
edge of armhole.
1st row P 1, * K1, P1, rep from * to
end.
2nd row K1, * P1, K1, rep from * to
end.
3rd row As first row.
4th row Using A, as 2nd row.
5th row Using A, as first row.
6th row Using MC, as 2nd row.
7th row Using MC, as first row.
Bind off loosely in rib.

To finish
Join side seams and armhole bands.
Sew on buttons to correspond with
buttonholes.
Sew on pockets.
Press seams lightly on WS with
warm iron.

HELPING HAND

Working mitered corners
Mitered corners add a professional
touch to borders. They are made by
working increases on each side of
the corner stitch.

1 *Cast on the required number of
stitches. Purl the first row,
marking the corner corner stitch
with a colored thread. On the next
row, knit to the corner stitch, then
with the point of the left-hand
needle, pick up the stitch below the
stitch just knitted into and knit it.
Knit the corner stitch in the usual
way, then knit into the stitch in the*

*row below the next stitch but do
not slip the loop off the left-hand
needle. Knit into the loop on the
left-hand needle and slip the loop
off the needle. Repeat these two
increases at every corner. Purl the
next row.*

2 *Work corner increases on every
right-side row until border is
desired length, ending with a
wrong side row. For rounded
corner, bind off in usual way. For
squared corner, bind off, increasing
at each side of corner stitch.*

Striped Yoke Pullover

This striped yoke pullover with crew neck would suit a girl or a boy equally well. The one-piece yoke is made in rounds.

Sizes
To fit 22[24]" chest
Length 13¾[15¼]"
Sleeve seam 11¾[13]"
Note Instructions for larger size are in brackets [ ]; where there is only one set of figures it applies to both sizes.

Materials
☐ 6[7] oz of a sport weight yarn in main color MC
☐ Small amount in each of 3 contrasting colors A, B and C
☐ One pair each of sizes 3 and 6 knitting needles
☐ One size 6 circular knitting needle 16" long
☐ Set of four each sizes 3 and 6 double-pointed knitting needles

Gauge
22 sts and 26 rows to 4" over St st using size 6 needles.

To save time, take time to check gauge.

Back
Using smaller needles and MC, cast on 68[74] sts. Work in K1, P1 rib for 1½″, ending with a WS row. Change to larger needles and beg with a K row, work in St st until back measures 8½[9½]″ from beg, ending with a P row.

Shape raglan armholes
Bind off 3 sts at beg of next 2 rows. Dec one st at each end of next row and then every other row until 52 sts rem. Leave sts on a spare needle.

Front
Work as for back.

Sleeves (make 2)
Using smaller needles and MC, cast on 32[36] sts. Work in K1, P1 rib for 2″, ending with a WS row. Change to larger needles and beg with a K row, work in St st for 4 rows.
Inc one st at each end of next row and then every 6th row until there are 52[58] sts and sleeve measures 11¾[13]″, ending with a P row.

Shape raglan top
Bind off 3 sts at beg of next 2 rows. Dec one st each end of next row and then every other row until 36 sts rem. Place these sts on a spare needle.

Yoke
With circular needle and MC, K36 sts from top of first sleeve, 52 sts from top of front, 36 sts from top of 2nd sleeve and 52 sts from top of back. 176 sts.
Work in rounds (i.e. every row K). When working with circular needle becomes difficult, change to a set of size 6 double-pointed needles.
Next round Using MC, (K2 tog, K9) 16 times.
Join in A and K 2 rounds, then K one round MC.
Next round Using MC, (K2 tog, K8) 16 times.
Join in A and K 2 rounds, then K one round MC.
Next round Using MC, (K2 tog, K7) 16 times.
Join in C and K 2 rounds, then K one round MC.

HELPING HAND

Working a circular yoke
Tubular knitted garments with circular yokes are found among ethnic and traditional garments. Many countries have adopted this style·yoke and elaborated it with intricate patterns, as found in the Shetlands and Fair Isles of Scotland and in Scandinavia. Because there are no seams, patterns may be easily matched. Decreases may be arranged in many different ways to fit in with a particular pattern or design. On a stockinette stitch yoke it is usual to place the decreases in a decorative way – often in vertical lines. To do this the stitches between the decrease stitches are reduced in number every following row as required.

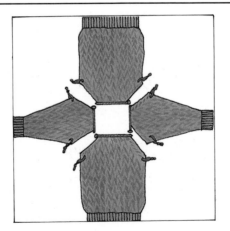

1 *Before the yoke can be worked the back, front and sleeve sections need to be completed. A short raglan section is worked at the top of each section and finished on the wrong side row. Mark the beginning of the raglan section with a colored thread at each end of the row on all four pieces.*

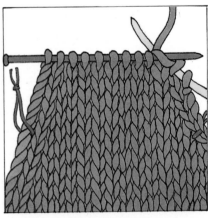

2 *Hold the stitches of one sleeve in the left hand. With the right side of the work facing, hold one point of the circular needle in the right hand. Knit across the stitches from the sleeve top.*

Next round Using MC, (K2 tog, K6) 16 times.
Join in A and K 2 rounds, then K one round MC.
Next round Using MC, (K2 tog, K5) 16 times.
Join in B and K 2 rounds, then K one round MC.
Next round Using MC, (K2 tog, K4) 16 times.
Join in C and K 2 rounds, then K one round MC.
Next round Using MC, (K2 tog, K3) 16 times.
Join in A and K 2 rounds, then K one round MC.

Neckband
Change to set of four size 6 double-pointed needles and work in K1, P1 rib for 2½".
Bind off very loosely in rib.

To finish
Join raglan seams. Join side and sleeve seams. Fold neckband in half and sew in place.
Press lightly on WS with warm iron.

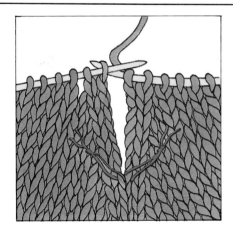

3 *Take the front section with the right side facing and hold it in the left hand. Knit across the stitches using the same point of the circular needle. Pull the yarn tightly when knitting the first stitch to avoid a hole.*

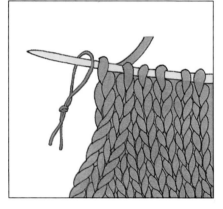

4 *In the same way, knit across the other sleeve and back section, transferring all the stitches onto the circular needle. Place a small loop of contrast colored yarn on the right-hand point of the needle. This will indicate the beginning of each round.*

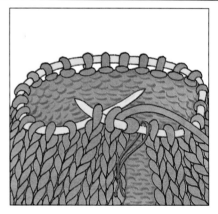

5 *Still holding the same end of the circular needle in the right hand, take the other end in the left hand and arrange the pieces of knitting along the length of the needle so that the right side of each section is facing outward. Using the same ball of yarn, begin knitting the stitches of the left-hand needle, thus joining the circle.*

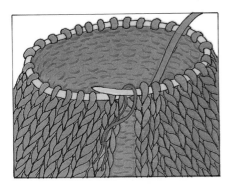

6 Continue to knit across all stitches until the colored marker has been reached. This indicates that a complete round has been worked. Slip the marker onto the right-hand needle and continue to knit the next round. Repeat this process at the end of the round, making sure the marker is always moved up on a new round.

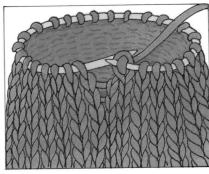

7 Continue to work in rounds, knitting all the time and working the first decrease round as instructed in the pattern.

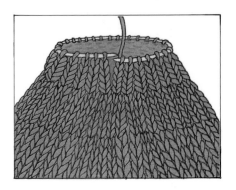

8 Knit in rounds until next decrease round is reached. This time the number of knitted stitches between the decreases will be one stitch less than in the previous round. The number of decreases still remains the same. As the rounds become shorter you will need to switch to a shorter circular needle or a set of double-pointed needles.

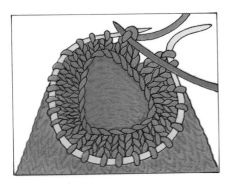

9 Continue working the decreases until the neckband has been reached. Now work on the smaller size circular needle or smaller size double-pointed needles, still leaving the colored marker. Continue to work across the stitches in rib until all the stitches have been transferred.

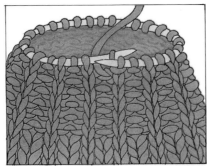

10 Work in rounds on the new set of needles as before. When the neckband is the required length, bind off the stitches in rib, making sure the end is securely fastened.

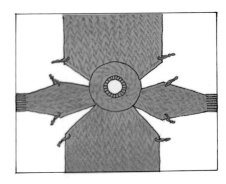

11 Before sewing the side and sleeve seams together, sew the raglan sections at the top of the front, back and sleeve sections.

Patterned Jacket

This sturdy zipped bomber jacket, decorated with multicolored panels in an abstract geometric design, is both smart and practical. Change the motifs to suit your taste.

Back

Using smaller needles and MC, cast on 77[83:89:95] sts.

1st row (RS) K1, *P1, K1, rep from * to end.

2nd row P1, *K1, P1, rep from * to end.

Rep last 2 rows until back measures 2″ from beg, ending with a first row.

Next row Rib 15[17:19:21], pick up strand between st just worked and next st and work into back of it – called M1 –, (rib 5, M1) twice, rib 27[29:31:33], (M1, rib 5) twice, M1, rib 15[17:19:21]. 83[89:95:101] sts. Change to larger needles and beg pat as foll:

Next row K9[11:13:15] MC, work first row from chart, K27[29:31:33] MC, work first row from chart, K9 [11:13:15] MC.

Next row P9[11:13:15] MC, work 2nd row from chart, P27[29:31:33] MC, work 2nd row from chart, P9 [11:13:15] MC.

These 2 rows set pat. Cont in pat as set, keeping chart correct until back measures 11¾[12¼:13¼:13]″ from beg, ending with a P row.

Shape armholes

Bind off 3[4:4:4] sts at beg of next 2 rows.

Dec one st at each end of next 3 rows, then every other row until 69[71:75:77] sts rem.

Work even until armholes measure 6[6¼:6¾:7]″ from beg, ending with a P row.

Shape shoulders

Bind off 7[7:8:8] sts at beg of next 4 rows and 8 sts at beg of next 2 rows.

Leave rem 25[27:27:29] sts on a st holder.

Sizes

To fit 26[28:30:32]″ chest
Length 17¾[18½:20:20]″
Sleeve seam 13[14:15½:17]″

Note Instructions for larger sizes are in brackets [ ]; where there is only one set of figures it applies to all sizes.

Materials

☐ 6[6:7:7]oz of a sport weight yarn in main color MC
☐ 3½oz in each of 3 contrasting colors A, B and C
☐ One pair each of sizes 3 and 6 knitting needles
☐ 18[18:20:20]″ open-ended zipper

Gauge

22 sts and 30 rows to 4″ over St st using size 6 needles.

To save time, take time to check gauge.

■ MC ■ B
■ A □ C

Patterned Jacket

Left front
Using smaller needles and MC, cast on 39[43:45:49] sts.
1st row (RS) *K1, P1, rep from * to last 3 sts, K3.
2nd row K2, P1, *K1, P1, rep from * to end.
Rep last 2 rows until front measures 2″ from beg, ending with a first row.
Next row Rib 15[17:18:20], M1, (rib 5, M1) twice, rib 14[16:17:19]. 42[46:48:52] sts.
Change to larger needles and beg pat as foll:
Next row K9[11:13:15] MC, work first row from chart, K14[16:16:18] MC.
Next row K2 MC, P12[14:14:16] MC, work 2nd row from chart, P9 [11:13:15] MC.
These 2 rows set pat. Cont in pat as set, keeping 2 sts in garter st at front edge and chart correct until 8 rows have been worked.
Divide for pocket
Next row Work 8[10:12:14] sts in pat, turn and leave rem sts on a st holder.
Next row Using MC, cast on 24 sts, P across these sts, P to end. 32[34: 36:38] sts.
Cont in St st, working 27 rows, ending with a K row and keeping chart correct.
Next row Bind off 24 sts, break off yarn and sl rem sts onto a st holder. With RS facing, rejoin yarn to sts on first st holder and work in pat to end. 34[36:36:38] sts.
Beg with a P row and keeping pat correct, work 28 rows.
Next row Work in pat to end, then work across sts on second st holder. 42[46:48:52] sts.
Cont until front measures same as back to armhole shaping, ending at side edge.
Shape armhole
Next row Bind off 3[4:4:4] sts, work in pat to end.
Next row Work to end.
*Dec one st at armhole edge on next 3 rows, then on every other row until 35[37:38:40] sts rem.

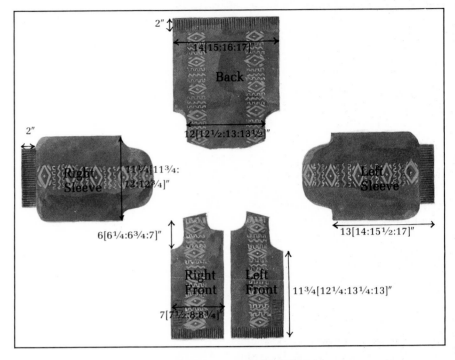

Work even until front measures 16 rows less than back to shoulder shaping, ending with a P row.*
Shape neck
Next row Work 26[26:28:28] sts in pat, K2 tog, turn and leave rem 7[9:8:10] sts on a safety pin. 27[27:29:29] sts.
Dec one st at neck edge on next 2 rows and and then on every other row 3 times. 22[22:24:24] sts.
Work even until front measures same as back to shoulder shaping, ending at armhole edge.
Shape shoulder
Bind off at armhole edge on every other row 7[7:8:8] sts twice and 8 sts once.

Right front
Using smaller needles and MC, cast on 39[43:45:49] sts.
1st row (RS) K3, *P1, K1, rep from * to end.
2nd row P1, *K1, P1, rep from * to last 2 sts, K2.
Rep last 2 rows until front measures 2″ from beg, ending with a first row.
Next row Rib 14[16:17:19], (M1, rib 5) twice, M1, rib 15[17:18:20]. 42

[46:48:52] sts.
Change to larger needles.
Next row K14[16:16:18] MC, work first row from chart, K9[11:13:15] MC.
Next row P9[11:13:15] MC, work 2nd row from chart, P12[14:14:16] MC, K2 MC.
These 2 rows establish pat. Work 6 more rows.
Divide for pocket
Next row Work 34[36:36:38] sts in pat, turn and leave rem sts on a st holder.
Beg with a P row and keeping pat correct, work 28 rows.
Break off yarn and leave sts on a st holder.
Return to sts on first st holder.
Using MC, cast on 24 sts, then with RS facing, K across sts on st holder. 32[34:36:38] sts.
Cont in St st and beg with a P row, work 27 rows.
Next row Bind off 24 sts, K to end.
Next row P8[10:12:14] MC, then work in pat across sts on 2nd st holder. 42[46:48:52] sts.
Cont until front matches back to armhole shaping, ending at armhole edge.

Shape armhole

Next row Bind off 3[4:4:4] sts, work to end.

Work as for left from from * to *.

Shape neck

Next row Work 7[9:8:10] sts in pat and leave these sts on a safety pin, K2 tog, work in pat to end. 27[27:29:29] sts.

Complete to match left front, reversing shaping.

Sleeves (make 2)

Using smaller needles and MC, cast on 41[41:43:43] sts. Work in K1, P1 rib as for back for 2″, ending with a first row.

Next row Rib 2[1:2:6], * rib 1, M1, rib 2[2:2:1], M1, rep from * to last 3[1:2:7] sts, rib to end. 65[67:69:73] sts.

Change to larger needles.

Next row K23[24:25:27] MC, work first row of chart, K23[24:25:27] MC.

Next row P23[24:25:27] MC, work 2nd row of chart, P23[24:25:27] MC.

These 2 rows establish pat. Cont in pat, keeping colors and chart correct until sleeve measures 13[14:15½:17]″ from beg, ending with a P row.

Shape cap

Bind off 3[4:4:4] sts at beg of next 2 rows.

Dec one st at each end of next row and then every other row until 37[29:29:29] sts rem, ending with a P row.

Dec one st at each end of every row until 21 sts rem.

Bind off.

Pocket edgings

With RS facing and using smaller needles and MC, pick up and K23 sts evenly along pocket edge. Work in K1, P1 rib as for back. Beg with 2nd row, work 7 rows.

Bind off loosely in rib.

Neckband

Join shoulder seams.

With RS facing and using smaller needles and MC, K across 7[9:8:10] sts on right front safety pin, pick up and K14 sts up right side of neck, K across 25[27:27:29] sts from back neck, pick up and K14 sts down left side of neck, K across 7[9:8:10] sts on left front safety pin. 67[73:71:77] sts.

1st row (WS) K2, P1, *K1, P1, rep from * to last 2 sts, K2.

2nd row K3, P1, *K1, P1, rep from * to last 3 sts, K3.

Rep last 2 rows until neckband measures 4″ from beg, ending with a first row.

Bind off very loosely in rib.

To finish

Join side and sleeve seams. Set in sleeves.

Sew down pocket linings and pocket edgings.

Fold neckband in half onto WS and sew down. Sew in zipper.

Press seams lightly on WS with warm iron.

HELPING HAND

Inserting a zipper

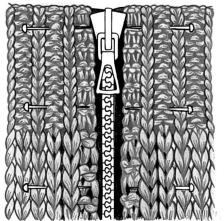

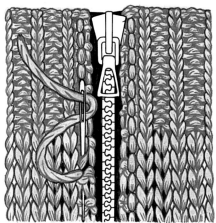

1 *Place the edges of the knitting right sides up level with the outside edges of the zipper teeth with the zipper closed. Be careful not to overlap the knitting onto the teeth.*

2 *Pin the zipper in position on both sides, easing the knitted fabric and stretching the zipper slightly to fit both sides exactly.*

3 *Using a matching thread, sew in the zipper with a backstitch seam worked close to the edge of the knitting.*

Patterned Jacket

Stepped border
This pattern has a bold
geometric feel. Work the middle
16 stitches on the chart only for
a border.

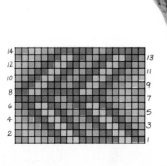

Zigzags
This pattern should be repeated
over 14 rows for a vertical border
and over 20 stitches for a
horizontal border. It can also be
used as an allover pattern.

Bird

This bird design occurs as a
motif in various forms in folk art
all over the world.

Cockerel

This splendid cockerel is
another traditional folk art
pattern which would make a fine
motif for decorating the jacket.

Dancers

These stylized human revelers
can be used as a single motif or
repeated to form a colorful
horizontal border.

Elephant and Kite Tops

Embroider a friendly family of elephants or a group of swirling kites onto the front of a basic round neck or V-neck sweater. Tie bows to the kites to add to the fun.

Sizes
Both versions:
To fit 24[26:28]″ chest
Length 17[17¾:18½]″
Sleeve seam 12½[14¼:15]″
Note Instructions for larger sizes are in brackets [ ]; where there is only one set of figures it applies to all sizes.

Materials
Elephant pullover:
☐ 9[9:11]oz of a sport weight yarn in main color MC (dark blue)
☐ Small amounts of white, black, yellow, gray, mid-blue, light blue and red
Kite pullover:
☐ 9[9:11]oz of a sport weight yarn in main color MC (red)
☐ Small amounts of white, black, yellow, green and blue
☐ One pair each of sizes 3 and 6 knitting needles
☐ Tapestry needle

Gauge
22 sts and 30 rows to 4″ over St st using size 6 needles.

To save time, take time to check gauge.

Elephant pullover

Back
* Using smaller needles and MC, cast on 74[80:86] sts. Work in K1, P1 rib for 2″.
Change to larger needles and cont in St st until back measures 10½[11:11½]″ from beg, ending with a WS row.
Shape armholes
Bind off 3[4:5] sts at beg of next 2 rows.
Dec one st at each end of next row and then every other row until 62[64:68] sts rem.*
Work even until armhole measures 6½[6¾:7]″, ending with a WS row.

Shape shoulders
Bind off 6[6:6] sts at beg of next 4 rows and 6[6:7] sts at beg of next 2 rows. Leave rem 26[28:30] sts on a st holder.

Front
Work as for back from * to *.
Work even until armhole measures 4¾[5:5]″, ending with a WS row.
Shape neck
Next row K24[25:26] sts, turn.
Next row P2 tog, P to end.
Dec one st at neck edge on every row until 18[18:19] sts rem.

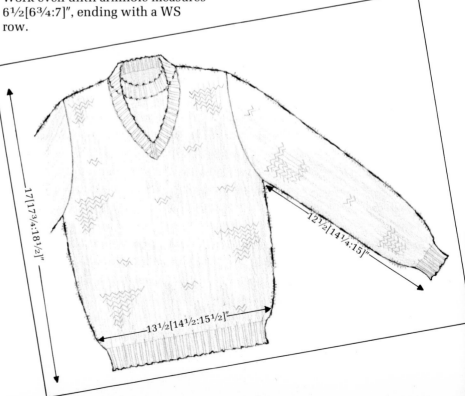

17[17¾:18½]″

12½[14¼:15]″

13½[14½:15½]″

Work even until front measures same as back to shoulder shaping, ending at armhole edge.

Shape shoulder
Bind off at armhole edge on every other row 6[6:6] sts twice and 6[6:7] sts once.

Second side of neck
With RS facing, sl center 14[14:16] sts onto a st holder, rejoin MC and K to end of row.
Next row P to last 2 sts, P2 tog.
Complete as for first side of neck, reversing all shaping.

Sleeves (make 2)
Using smaller needles and MC, cast on 36[38:38] sts. Work in K1, P1 rib for 2″.
Next row Rib 4[5:5], (pick up strand between st just worked and next st and work into back of it — called M1 —, rib 3) 10 times, rib to end. 46[48:48] sts.
Change to larger needles and cont in St st, inc one st at each end of 3rd row and then every 12th[13th:11th] row until there are 58[62:64] sts.
Work even until sleeve measures 12½[14¼:15]″ from beg, ending with a WS row.
Shape cap
Bind off 3[4:5] sts at beg of next 2 rows.
Dec one st at each end of next row and then every 4th row until there are 42[46:42] sts. Dec one st at each end of every other row until there are 34[34:36] sts. Dec one st at each end of every row until there are 20[20:22] sts.
Bind off.

Neckband
Join right shoulder seam.
With RS facing and using smaller needles and MC, pick up and K14[14:16] sts down left side of neck, K14[14:16] sts from center front, pick up and K14[14:16] sts up right side of neck and K26[28:30] sts from back neck inc 8 sts evenly. 76[78:86] sts.
Work 7 rows in K1, P1 rib.

Bind off loosely in rib.

To finish
Foll chart, embroider elephants across front, using duplicate st (see page 94).
Work tails and ears in chain st (see page 163). Work tusks, toes and eyes in satin st (see page 162).

Join shoulder, neckband, side and sleeve seams. Set in sleeves. Press lightly on WS with warm iron.

Kite pullover

Back
Work as for elephant pullover.

Elephant and Kite Tops

Front
Using smaller needles and MC, cast on 75[81:87] sts. Work in K1, P1 rib for 2".
Change to larger needles and cont in St st until front measures same as back to armholes, ending with a WS row.

Shape armholes and divide for neck
Bind off 3[4:5] sts at beg of next 2 rows.
Next row K2 tog, K 30[32:34], K2 tog, turn.
P one row.
Dec one st at armhole edge of next row and then every other row and *at the same time*, dec one st at neck edge on every 3rd row until 29[29:31] sts rem. Cont to dec at neck edge as before until 18[18:19] sts rem.
Work even until front measures same as back to shoulder shaping, ending at armhole edge.

Shape shoulder
Bind off at armhole edge on every row 6[6:6] sts twice and 6[6:7] sts once.

Second side of neck
With RS facing, sl center st onto a safety pin, join in MC, K2 tog, K to last 2 sts, K2 tog.
P one row.
Complete as for first side of neck, reversing all shaping.

Sleeves (make 2)
Work as for elephant pullover.

Neckband
Join right shoulder seam.
With RS facing and using smaller needles and MC, pick up and K48[50:52] sts up right side of neck, K26[28:30] sts from back neck inc 8 sts evenly, pick up and K48[50:52] sts down left side of neck, K st on safety pin and mark it. 131[137:143] sts.
1st row Work in K1, P1 rib to within 2 sts of marked st, P2 tog, P1, P2 tog, rib to end.
2nd row Rib to within 2 sts of marked st, sl 1-K1-psso, K1, K2 tog, rib to end.
Rep these 2 rows twice, then first row once.
Bind off in rib, dec as before.

To finish
Foll chart, embroider kites across front, using duplicate st.
Work ribs of kites in chain st (see page 163) and kite tails in stem st (see page 78).
Sew bows to kites and tails as desired.
Complete as for elephant pullover.

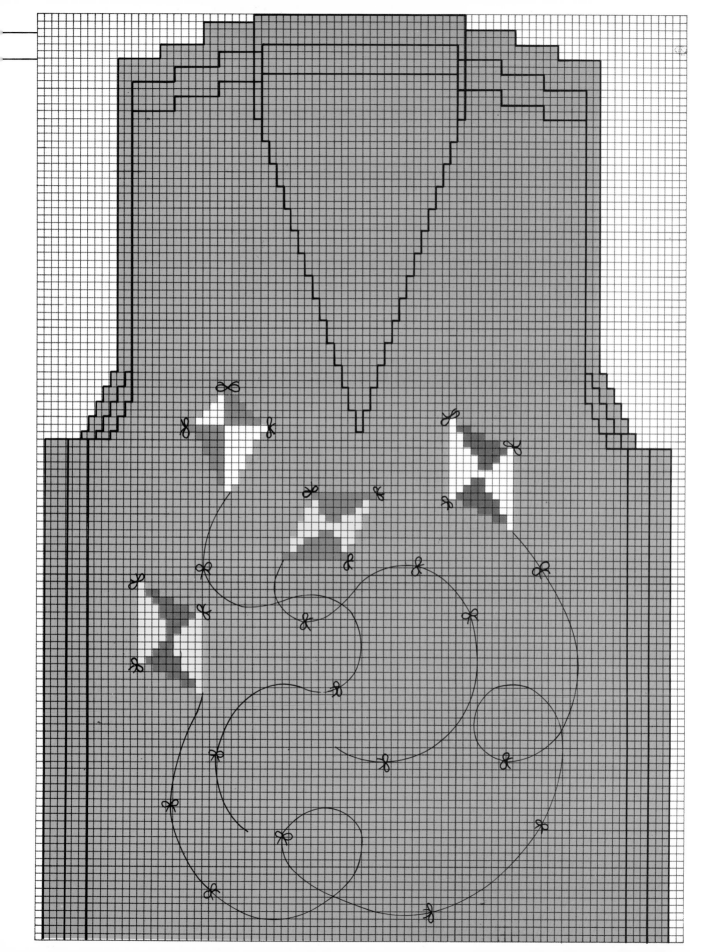

Trompe l'Oeil V-neck

The special technique used on the V-neckline creates a clever trick-of-the-eye effect. Instead of being worked along the edge of the neck, the decreases for the "V" are worked along the edge of the zipper panel.

Size
To fit 30-32″ chest
Length 18½″
Sleeve seam 16½″

Materials
☐ 13oz of a sport weight yarn in main color MC
☐ 1¾oz in contrasting color A
☐ One pair each of sizes 3 and 5 knitting needles
☐ Set of four size 3 double-pointed knitting needles

Gauge
22 sts and 32 rows to 4″ over St st using size 5 needles.

To save time, take time to check gauge.

Note When working zipper pat, use a separate ball of MC for each side so that MC does not have to be stranded behind A. When changing color, twist yarns to avoid holes.

Back and front
Back and front are worked in one piece, beg at lower front edge. Using smaller needles and MC, cast on 82 sts. Work 19 rows in K1, P1 rib.
Change to larger needles.
Next row P to end, inc 13 sts evenly across row. 95 sts.
Beg zipper pat as foll:

Join in A and beg working in St st foll chart 1, reading K rows from right to left and P rows from left to right.
1st row K30 MC, work first row of chart, K30 MC.
2nd row P30 MC, work 2nd row of chart, P30 MC.
These 2 rows establish the position

of zipper pat. Cont in this way until 82 rows have been worked from chart.

Divide for neck

Next row With MC, (K3, work twice into next st – called inc 1) 3 times, K12, K2 tog, K22, sl these 50 sts onto a st holder, K21, sl 1-K1-psso, K12, (inc 1, K3) 3 times. Complete right side of neck first. With MC, work 3 rows in St st. Beg working from chart 2 as foll:

Next row Work first row of chart 2, sl 1-K1-psso, K to end.

Next row P to last 21 sts, work 2nd row of chart 2.

Next row Work 3rd row of chart, K to end.

Next row P to last 21 sts, work 4th row of chart.

Next row Work 5th row of chart, sl 1-K1-psso, K to end.

**Cont in this way and keeping chart correct (rep the 12 rows throughout), dec one st as before on every 4th row until 38 sts rem, ending with the dec row. Work even for 5 rows, ending with a P row. ** Leave these sts on a st holder.

Return to sts on other st holder. With WS facing, sl center st onto a safety pin, join in MC to next st and beg with a P row, work 3 rows in St st.

Beg working from chart 3 as foll:

Next row K to last 23 sts, K2 tog, work first row of chart 3.

Next row Work 2nd row of chart 3, P to end.

Next row K to last 21 sts, work 4th row of chart.

Next row K to last 23 sts, K2 tog, work 5th row of chart.

Cont as for first side of neck from ** to **.

Next row Work across these 38 sts, cast on 19 sts, then work across sts for right side of neck. 95 sts. Work one row to complete zipper.

Back

Cont in MC only, beg with a K row and work 130 rows in St st.

Next row K to end, dec 13 sts evenly across row. 82 sts.

Change to smaller needles and work 19 rows in K1, P1 rib. Bind off in rib.

Sleeves (make 2)

Using smaller needles and MC, cast on 40 sts. Work 18 rows in K1, P1 rib.

Change to larger needles.

Next row K to end, inc 8 sts evenly across row. 48 sts.

Beg with a P row, cont in St st, inc one st at each end of every 8th row until there are 70 sts.

Work even until 122 rows have been worked in St st, ending with a P row.

Bind off.

Neckband

With RS facing and using three of set of double-pointed needles and MC, pick up and K30 sts down right side of neck, K center st from safety pin, pick up and K30 sts up left side of neck and 19 sts across back neck. 80 sts.

Work in rounds as foll:

1st round Work in K1, P1 rib to within one st of center st, sl 2-K1-p2sso, rib to end.

Rep last round 7 times more.

Bind off loosely in rib, dec on this round as before.

To finish

Join side and sleeve seams. Set in sleeves. Press lightly on WS with warm iron.

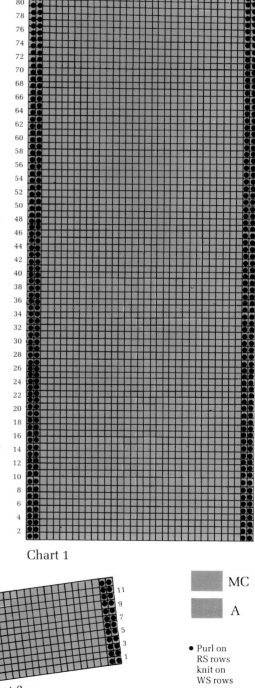

Chart 1

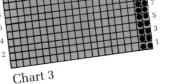

Chart 2

Chart 3

MC

A

• Purl on RS rows knit on WS rows

Chapter 3
DRESSES & OVERALLS

The dresses and overalls given here are some of the prettiest and most practical additions you could make to any little girl's wardrobe. You can choose between the sweetest party dresses shaped on classic lines with frilled and scalloped edgings, to fit chest sizes 18″ – 24″, and easy-styled overalls in bright, sporty colors for playtime and weekend wear, to fit chest sizes 20″ – 25″.

Stitch patterns include charted colorwork, as in the Sampler Dress and the picture patch overalls on pages 99 and 115. There are also lacy patterns, picot edgings, and honeycomb smocking (see pages 102, 105 and 108) in fact, so many attractive details and finishes little girls will simply adore.

Sampler Dress

This patterned dress is made in two main parts. The skirt is knitted on a circular needle and the top is worked sideways from one cuff to the other.

Sizes
To fit 22[24]" chest
Length 20½[21¼]"
Note Instructions for larger size are in brackets [ ]; where there is only one set of figures it applies to both sizes.

Materials
☐ 7[9]oz of a sport weight yarn in main color MC
☐ 1¾oz in each of 9 contrasting color A, B, C, D, E, F, G, H and J
☐ One size 5 circular knitting needle
☐ One pair each of sizes 3 and 5 knitting needles

Gauge
22 sts and 28 rows to 4" over St st using size 5 needles.

To save time, take time to check gauge.

Skirt

Using circular needle and MC, cast on 240[252] sts. Work in rounds as foll:

K one round. P 4 rounds.

Next round * K3 B, P3 MC, rep from * to end.

Cont in St st (K every round) and work first 18th rounds foll chart A.

19th round (dec round) Using A, K5[19], K2 tog, * K10[23], K2 tog, rep from * to last 5[6] sts, K5[6] sts. 220[242] sts.

Work 20th and 35th rounds foll chart B.

36th round (dec round) * Using MC, K2 tog, K8[9], rep from * to end. 198[220] sts.

Using MC, work 11 rounds in St st.

48th round (dec round) Using MC, K6[5], K2 tog, * K9[8], K2 tog, rep from * to last 3 sts, K3. 180[198] sts.

Work 49th to 59th rounds foll chart C.

60th round (dec round) Using MC, K9[8], K2 tog, * K13[9], K2 tog, rep from * to last 4[1] sts, K4[1]. 168[180] sts.

Using MC, work 2 rounds in St st. Foll chart for Bird's eye pat, work even until 20[30] rounds of pat have been completed. Skirt measures approx 12¼[13½]″.

Using MC, work 14[10] rows in St st.

Dec row Using MC, ** K2 tog, K3, K4 tog, (K3, K3[4] tog) twice, K21[22] and leave a marker here for side seam **, *K21[22], (K3[4] tog, K3) twice, K4 tog, K3, K2 tog *, rep from ** to ** once, then from * to * once. 136[140] sts rem.

K one round.

Bind off firmly. Skirt measures 24½[25¼]″ all around top.

Sleeves and bodice

Using smaller needles and MC, cast on 36[38] sts. Work in K1, P1 rib for 8 rows.

Next row (inc row) K4[5], * pick up strand between st just worked and next st and K into back of it – called M1 –, rep from * to last 5[6] sts, M1, K5[6]. 46[48] sts.

Change to larger needles and cont in St st beg with a P row and

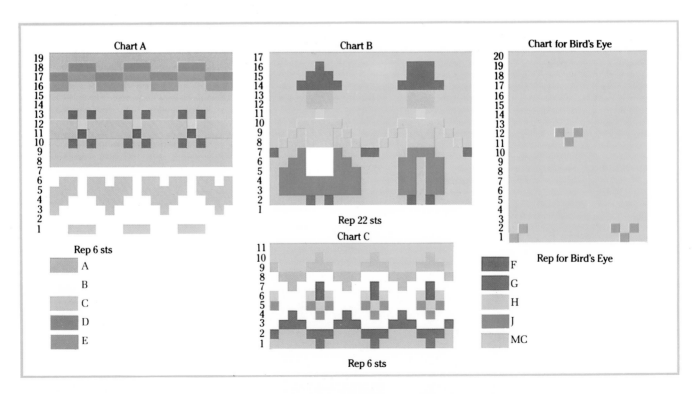

Chart A	Chart B	Chart for Bird's Eye
19 18 17 16 15 14 13 12 11 10 9 8 7 6 5 4 3 2 1	17 16 15 14 13 12 11 10 9 8 7 6 5 4 3 2 1	20 19 18 17 16 15 14 13 12 11 10 9 8 7 6 5 4 3 2 1
Rep 6 sts	Rep 22 sts	Rep for Bird's Eye

Chart C

11 10 9 8 7 6 5 4 3 2 1

Rep 6 sts

A
B
C
D
E

F
G
H
J
MC

working 3 rows in pat foll chart C, and *at the same time* shape sleeve by inc one st at each end of 3rd[5th] row, then next two 5th[3rd] rows and then at each end of every 5th row until there are 70[76] sts.
Work 5[4] rows in St st.
Using MC, work 4 rows in St st.
Working even, position pat foll chart C as foll:
Next row K2[5] MC, K1 G, * K5 MC, K1 G, rep from * to last 1[4] sts, K1[4] MC.
Work next 9 rows of chart C.
Using MC, work 4 rows in St st.
Work 2 rows of Bird's eye pat, positioning first row as foll:
Next row K8[11] MC, K1 E, * K11 MC, K1 E, rep from * to last 1[4] sts, K1[4] MC.
Work 2nd row of Bird's eye foll chart.
Using MC, work 8 rows in St st.
Work 2 rows of Bird's eye, positioning it between last pat.
Using MC, K one row.

Divide for neck
Next row P35[38] sts, turn and leave rem 35[38] sts on a st holder.
Cont on these 35[38] sts, work 6 rows in St st.
Work 2 rows Bird's eye pat, positioning it between last pat.
Using MC, work 7 rows in St st.

Buttonhole band
Change to smaller needles and beg rib as foll:
Next row P1[0], (K1, P1) to end.
Next row (RS) * Rib 5, yo, work 2 tog, rep from * 4 times, rib 7[10].
Next row Rib to end.
Bind off loosely in rib.

Left back
Using smaller needles and MC, cast on 35[38] sts.
Next row P1[0], (K1, P1) to end.
Next row (K1, P1) to last 1[0] sts, K1[0].
Rep last 2 rows once.
Change to larger needles and work 7 rows in St st, using MC.
Work 2 rows of Bird's eye to match last Bird's eye rows of right back.
Work 8 rows in St st.
Break off yarn and leave these sts

on a st holder until later.
Front neck
Rejoin MC at back neck and bind off 8 sts, P to end.
1st row K to last 2 sts, K2 tog.
2nd row P to end.
Rep these 2 rows twice more.
Next row Poisition Bird's eye between last Bird's eye rows to last 2 sts, K2 tog.
Next row P to end, working Bird's eye pat.
Rep first and 2nd rows 3 times more. 20[23] sts.
Using MC, work 2 rows in St st, then work 2 more rows of Bird's eye between last pat. Using MC, work 4 more rows.
23rd row K to end, inc one st at end of row.
24th row P to end.
Rep these 2 rows once more.
Next row K to end, working Bird's eye pat and inc one st at end of row.
Next row P to end, working Bird's eye pat.
Work 23rd and 24th rows 4 times more.
Next row Working Bird's eye, K to end, cast on 8 sts, K across sts for left back. 70[76] sts.
Left sleeve
Next row P to end, working Bird's eye pat.
Using MC, work 8 rows in St st.
Work 2 more rows of Bird's eye pat.
Using MC, work 4 rows in St st.
Work foll chart C in reverse as foll:
Next row K2[5] MC, K1 A, * K5 MC, K1 A, rep from * to last 1[4] sts, K1[4] MC.
Cont for next 9 rows of reversed chart.
Using MC, work 8[7] rows in St st.
Dec one st at each end of next row and then every 5th row until there are 52[54] sts.
Using MC, work 3[2] rows in St st.
Work chart C in reverse as foll:
Next row K4[5] MC, K1 A, * K5 MC, K1 A, rep from * to last 5[0] sts, K5[0] MC.
Cont for next 9 rows of reversed chart.

Using MC, work 3 rows in St st, and *at the same time* dec one st at each end of 2nd[3rd] row and then 5th[3rd] rows twice. 46[48] sts.
Dec row P0[1], P2 tog, P2[3], * P2 tog, P3, rep from * to last 2 sts, P2 tog. 36[38] sts.
Change to smaller needles and MC.
Work in K1, P1 rib for 8 rows.
Bind off in rib.

Collar
With RS facing and using smaller needles and MC, pick up and K73 sts evenly around neck edge.
Next row (WS)* K1 tbl, rep from * to end.
Next row K1, (P1, K1) to end.
Next row P1, (K1, P1) to end.
Rep last 2 rows 8 times more.
Bind off.

To finish
Press pieces lightly on WS with warm iron.
Gather the skirt to fit between the center of the bands of pattern C, which defines the yoke. Sew skirt to bodice overlapping ribs at back bodice opening.
Sew sleeve seams.
Sew on buttons.

Party Dress

Dress your baby in this pretty party dress for an important day. It is with a multi-colored scalloped hem and embroidered at random with dainty flowers.

Sizes
To fit 18[20]" chest
Length 22½"
Sleeve seam 6[6¾]"
Note Instructions for larger size are in brackets [ ]; where there is only one set of figures it applies to both sizes.

Materials
☐ 12[14]oz of a fingering weight yarn in main color MC
☐ 1½oz in each of 3 contrasting colors A, B and C
☐ One pair of size 3 knitting needles
☐ 4 small buttons
☐ Tapestry needle

Gauge
26 sts and 34 rows to 4" over St st using size 3 needles.

To save time, take time to check gauge.

Note The lace pattern has been set over the first few rows. Make sure when working any shapings that the lace pattern is worked on the correct stitches.

Front
Using A, cast on 164[182] sts. K one row and beg scallop pat as foll:
1st row (RS) K1, (K2 tog) 3 times, * (yo, K1) 6 times, (K2 tog) 6 times, rep from * to last 13 sts, (yo, K1) 6 times, (K2 tog) 3 times, K1.
2nd row P to end.
3rd row P to end.
4th row Join in MC, P to end.
5th row As first row.
6th row As 2nd row.
7th row As 3rd row.
8th row Join in B and P to end.
These 8 rows form scallop pat.
Cont in pat, changing color every 4 rows in the sequence of 4 rows B, 4 rows MC, 4 rows C, 4 rows MC, 4 rows A, 4 rows MC, 4 rows B, 4 rows MC, 4 rows C.
Then change to MC and work 3 rows of pat only. Work 8 rows in St st then beg eyelet pat as foll:
1st row K18, * yo, sl 1-K1-psso, K16, rep from * to last 2 sts, K2.
2nd and every other row P to end.
3rd row K16, * K2 tog, yo, K1, yo, sl 1-K1-psso, K13, rep from * to last 4 sts, K4.
5th row K15, * K2 tog, yo, K3, yo, sl 1-K1-psso, K11, rep from * to last 5 sts, K5.
7th row K14, * K2 tog, yo, K5, yo, sl 1-K1-psso, K9, rep from * to last 6 sts, K6.
8th row P to end.
Work 10 rows in St st.
19th row K9, * yo, sl 1-K1-psso, K16, rep from *, ending last rep K9.
20th and every other row P to end.
21st row K7, * K2 tog, yo, K1, yo, sl 1-K1-psso, K13, rep from *, ending last rep K8.
23rd row K6, * K2 tog, yo, K3, yo, sl 1-K1-psso, K11, rep from *,

ending last rep K7.
25th row K5, * K2 tog, yo, K5, yo, sl 1-K1-psso, K9, rep from *, ending last rep K6.
26th row P to end.
Work 10 rows in St st beg with a K row.
These 36 rows form pat, rep until skirt measures 18" from beg, ending with a WS row.
Next row (K2 tog) 8[5] times, (K3 tog) 44[54] times, (K2 tog) 8[5] times. 60[64] sts.
Work 3 rows in St st.
Cont in pat as foll:
Next row K11[13], * yo, sl 1-K1-psso, K16, rep from *, ending last rep K11[13].
Next row P to end.

Shape armholes
Cont in pat as for skirt and keeping pat correct, shape armholes as foll:
Bind off 2 sts at beg of next 2 rows, then dec one st at each end of every other row until 52[56] sts rem.
Cont in pat until front measures 21¼" from beg.

Shape neck
Next row Work across 21[23] sts in pat, turn and leave rem sts on a st holder. Keeping armhole edge even, dec one st at neck edge on every row until 16[18] sts rem.
Cont working even until front measures 22½" from beg, ending at armhole edge.

Shape shoulders
Bind off 4 sts at beg of next row and every other row twice more.
Work one row.
Bind off rem 4[6] sts.
Rejoin yarn to sts on st holder and work one row in pat.
Next row P across 21[23] sts, P2 tog, turn and leave rem 10 sts on st

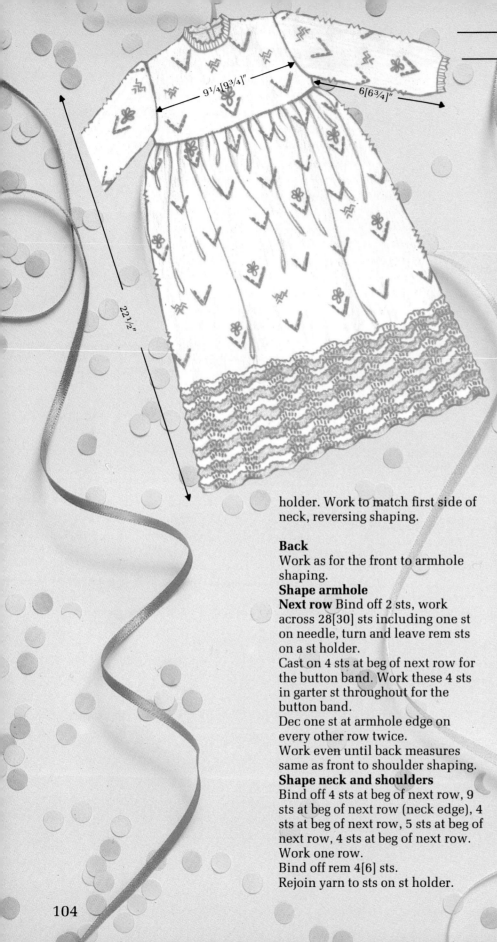

9¼[9¾]"

6[6¾]"

22½"

Cast on 4 sts at beg of first row for buttonhole band. Work to match first side of back, working a buttonhole on the 5th (RS row) and every foll 8th row as foll:
Buttonhole row K2, yo, K2 tog, work to end.

Sleeves (make 2)
Using MC, cast on 32[36] sts. Work in St st for 6 rows.
Picot row K1, * yo, K2 tog, rep from *, ending with K1.
Work 7 more rows in St st.
Inc row K3, (pick up strand between st just worked and next st and K into back of it, K2) 14[16] times, K1. 46[52] sts.
Work 9 rows in St st. Then work in pat as for front, beg with first pat row with K13[16] and working all foll rows to correspond.
Work even until sleeve measures 6[6¾]" from picot row.
Shape sleeve cap
Bind off 2 sts at beg of next 4 rows.
Dec one st at each end of next row and then every other row 5 times. 26[32] sts.
Bind off 3 sts at beg of next 4 rows.
Bind off rem 14[20] sts.

Neckband
Sew shoulder seams.
Using A, pick up and K59 sts around neck. Work 5 rows in St st, ending with a WS row.
Picot row K1, * yo, K2 tog, rep from * to end.
Work 5 more rows in St st.
Bind off loosely.

To finish
Fold neckband to WS; sew in place.
Sew side and sleeve seams.
Fold sleeve hems to WS and sew in place.
Set in sleeves, gathering in any fullness at top.
Sew on buttons to correspond with buttonholes.
Using contrasting colors and lazy daisy st (see page 78), embroider flowers at random in eyelet V's on back and front.

holder. Work to match first side of neck, reversing shaping.

Back
Work as for the front to armhole shaping.
Shape armhole
Next row Bind off 2 sts, work across 28[30] sts including one st on needle, turn and leave rem sts on a st holder.
Cast on 4 sts at beg of next row for the button band. Work these 4 sts in garter st throughout for the button band.
Dec one st at armhole edge on every other row twice.
Work even until back measures same as front to shoulder shaping.
Shape neck and shoulders
Bind off 4 sts at beg of next row, 9 sts at beg of next row (neck edge), 4 sts at beg of next row, 5 sts at beg of next row, 4 sts at beg of next row.
Work one row.
Bind off rem 4[6] sts.
Rejoin yarn to sts on st holder.

Picot Dress

This pretty baby's dress, with an unusual square neckline, is made using a washable yarn in a soft pastel color. The multiple picot edgings worked in snowy white resemble lace trim.

Sizes
To fit 18[20:22]″ chest
Length 11¾[14:16]″
Sleeve seam 2½″
Note Instructions for larger sizes are in brackets [ ]; where there is only one set of figures it applies to all sizes.

Materials
☐ 5[5:6]oz of a fingering weight yarn in main color MC
☐ 1[1:2]oz in a contrasting color A
☐ One pair each of sizes 2, 3 and 4 knitting needles
☐ Size B crochet hook
☐ 2 small buttons

Gauge
28 sts and 36 rows to 4″ over St st using size 4 needles.

To save time, take time to check gauge.

Picot Dress

Back

Using size 3 needles and a small length of A, cast on 119[125:131] sts loosely. (This cast-on edge will later be removed.)

Change to MC and work 4 rows in St st, beg with a K row.

Change to size 2 needles and A.

Next row K2, * yo, K2 tog, rep from * to last st, K1.

Next row P to end.

Change to size 3 needles and MC, beg with a K row and work 4 rows in St st.

Pull out the cast-on edge and place sts on a size 3 needle.

With WS of work tog, K one st from top edge and one st from lower edge tog as foll:

Next row * K1 MC, K1 A, rep from * to last st, K1 MC.

Next row * P1 A, P1 MC, rep from * to last st, P1 A.

Break off A.

**Using MC, work 4 rows in St st, beg with a K row.

Next row K to end, marking each end with a colored thread.

Work 3 rows in St st, beg with a P row.

Change to size 2 needles and A.

Next row K2, * yo, K2 tog, rep from * to last st, K1.

Next row P to end.

Change to size 3 needles and MC and work 4 rows in St st.

Using a size 3 needle, pick up the loops on the WS from the row marked with colored threads and with WS tog, work one st from each needle as foll:

Next row * K1 MC, K1 A, rep from * to last st, K1 MC.

Next row * P1 A, P1 MC, rep from * to last st, P1 A. **

Rep from ** to ** once.

Change to size 4 needles and cont in MC, work as foll:

Work 4 rows in St st, beg with a P row.

***Next row** K11[8:5], P1, * K11, P1, rep from * to last 11[8:5] sts, K to end.

Work 5 rows in St st, beg with a P row.

Next row K5[2:11], P1, * K11, P1, rep from * to last 5[2:11] sts, K to end.

Work 5 rows in St st.

Rep from *** until back measures 6½[8:9½]" from beg, ending with a K row.

Work dec row as foll:

First size only

Dec row P1, (P2 tog) 4 times, [P1, (P2 tog) 4 times] 11 times, P1, (P2 tog) 4 times, P2. 67 sts.

2nd size only

Dec row P2, (P2 tog) twice, [P1, (P2 tog) 3 times] 16 times, P1, (P2 tog) twice, P2. 73 sts.

3rd size only

Dec row P1, P2 tog, [P1, (P2 tog) twice] 25 times, P2 tog, P1. 79 sts.

All sizes

Rep from ** to ** twice.

Using size 4 needles and MC, work even until back measures 8¼ [10:11½]" from beg, working the pat on the first sequence with 9[12:9] sts at each end, the 2nd sequence with 3[6:3] sts at each end, ending with a WS.

Shape armholes

Bind off 8[9:10] sts at beg of next 2

rows. 51[55:59] sts.
Keeping pat correct, work even
until armhole measures 3½[4:4½]".
Shape shoulders
Bind off 8 sts at beg of next 2 rows,
then 7[8:9] sts at beg of next 2
rows.
Leave rem 21[23:25] sts on a st
holder.

Front
Work as for back to end of armhole
shaping.
Work even until front measures 18
rows less than back to shoulder
shaping.
Shape neck
Next row Work 15[16:17] sts in pat
and leave rem sts on a st holder.
Work even on these 15[16:17] sts,
until front measures same as back
to shoulder shaping, ending at
armhole edge.
Shape shoulder
Bind off 8 sts at beg of next row.
Work one row. Bind off 7[8:9] sts.
Shape second side of neck
Return to rem sts and with RS
facing, sl center 21[23:25] sts onto a
st holder, join in yarn to next st and
work to match first side of neck,
reversing shaping.

Sleeves (make 2)
Using size 2 needles and MC, cast
on 39[45:51] sts. Work in K1, P1 rib
for 7 rows.
Change to size 4 needles and beg
with a K row, work 4 rows in St st,
inc one st at each end of the 3rd
row. 41[47:53] sts.
Next row K8[11:8], P1, *K11, P1,
rep from * to last 8[11:8] sts, K to
end. Work 5 rows in St st, inc one st
at each end of first and 3rd rows.
45[51:57] sts.
Next row K4[7:4], P1, * K11, P1,
rep from * to last 4[7:4] sts, K to
end.
Next row P to end, inc one st at
each end of row. 47[53:59] sts.
Work 4 rows in St st. Place a
marker at each end of last row.
Keeping pat correct, work
10[12:14] more rows. Bind off.

Neckband
Join right shoulder seam.
With RS facing and using size 3
needles and A, pick up and K16 sts
down left front neck, K21[23:25] sts
from center front neck, pick up and
K16 sts up right front neck,
K21[23:25] sts from back neck.
74[78:82] sts.
Next row P to end.
Next row K1, * yo, K2 tog, rep from
* to center front, K2 tog, (yo, K2
tog) across center sts, K2 tog, * yo,
K2 tog, rep from * to last st, K1.
Next row P to end.

Work 4 rows in St st.
Bind off

To finish
Join left shoulder. Set in sleeves for
½" only. Join side and sleeve
seams.
Fold neckband and hem to WS and
sew down.
With crochet hook and MC, work a
row of single crochet around left
shoulder opening, making 2 loops
for buttonholes (see page 161).
Sew on buttons to match
buttonholes.

*The picot dress showing an easy-
fitting bodice. It has a buttoned
shoulder opening, a square neck
line, and deep inset sleeves.*

Smocked Dress

The smocking on this pretty dress is worked once the garment is completed. The lace ruffle in a contrasting color is stitched to the picot hem to add a delicate touch.

Sizes

To fit 20[22:24]″ chest
Length 15¾[17¾:19½]″
Sleeve seam 8¼[9½:10½]″
Note Instructions for larger sizes are in brackets [ ]; where there is only one set of figures it applies to all sizes.

Materials

☐ 7[8:10]oz of a sport weight yarn in main color MC
☐ 1½[2:2]oz in contrasting color A
☐ One pair of size 6 knitting needles
☐ Size E crochet hook
☐ Tapestry needle

Gauge

24 sts and 32 rows to 4″ over St st using size 6 needles.

To save time, take time to check gauge.

Back

**Using MC, cast on 114[120:126] sts. Work 4 rows in St st.
Next row K1, * yo, K2 tog, rep from * to last st, K1.
Cont in St st, dec one st at each end of every 10th[11th:12th] row 6 times in all. 102[108:114] sts.
Cont in St st until back measures 9[10¼:11½]″ from picot edge, ending with a WS row.

Shape armholes

Bind off 2 sts at beg of next 2 rows.
Dec one st at each end of next 5[6:7] rows.
Work one row.
Dec one st at each end of next row and then every other row until 84[88:92] sts rem. Work one row.
Dec row (P0[1:3], P2 tog) 3[4:8] times, (P1[2:4], P2 tog) 24[16:2] times, (P0[1:3], P2 tog) 3[4:8] times. 54[64:74] sts.
Work in rib pat as foll:
1st row P4, * K1, P4, rep from * to end.
2nd row K4, * P1, K4, rep from * to end.
Cont in pat for 2¾[3:3½]″, ending with a WS row. **

Divide for back neck opening

Next row Working in St st, K across first 27[32:37] sts, turn and leave rem 27[32:37] sts on a st holder.
Cont on first group of sts for 1½[2¼:3]″, ending with WS row.

Shape shoulders

Bind off 5[6:7] sts at beg of next row and then every other row twice.
Leave rem 12[14:16] sts on a st holder for neck edging.
Pick up 27[32:37] sts from first st holder and work as for first back neck, reversing shaping.

Front

Work as for back from ** to **, ending with a WS row.

Shape neck

Next row K across 20[24:28] sts, turn and leave rem 34[40:46] sts on a st holder.
Dec one st at beg of next row (neck edge) and then at neck edge on next 2[3:4] rows.
Work one row.
Dec one st at neck edge on every other row until 15[18:21] sts rem.
Cont on these sts until armhole measures same as back to shoulder shaping, ending with a WS row.

Shape shoulders

Bind off 5[6:7] sts at beg of next row and then every other row twice more.

Shape second side of neck

With RS facing, sl first 14[16:18] sts onto a st holder.
Cont on rem 20[24:28] sts and work as for first side of neck, reversing shaping.

Sleeves (make 2)

Using A, cast on 34[40:46] sts.
Work 4 rows in St st.
Next row K1, * yo, K2 tog, rep from * to last st, K1.
Work 3 rows in St st.
Change to MC and work in rib pat as foll:
1st row P4[7:5], * K1, P4, rep from * to last 5[8:6] sts, K1, P4[7:5].
2nd row K4[7:5], P1, * K4, P1, rep from * to last 4[7:5] sts, K4[7:5]
Rep last 2 rows 6 times in all.
Inc row (K1, pick up strand between st just worked and next st and work into back of it – called M1 –) 10[7:4] times, (K2, M1) 6[12:18] times, (K1, M1) 10[7:4]

times, K2. 60[66:72] sts.
Cont in St st until sleeve measures
8¼[9½:10½]″ from picot edge,
ending with a WS row.

Shape cap
Bind off 2 sts at beg of next 2 rows.
Dec one st at each end of every
row 6[6:8] times.
Dec one st at each end of every
other row 4[5:6] times.
Bind off 3 sts at beg of next 4 rows.
Bind off rem 24[28:28] sts.

Neck edging
Join both shoulder seams.
With RS facing and using A, beg at
back neck opening and pick up and
K12[14:16] sts along left side of
back neck, 10[12:14] sts along left
side of front neck, K14[16:18] sts
from center neck, pick up and
K10[12:14] sts along right side of
neck, 12[14:16] sts along right of
back neck. 58[68:78] sts.
Work 3 rows in St st.

Next row K1, * yo, K2 tog, rep from
* to last st, K1.
Work another 4 rows in St st.
Bind off loosely.

Ruffle (make 2)
Using A, cast on 134[156:178] sts.
1st and 2nd rows K to end.
3rd row K1, * (K2 tog) twice, (yo,
K1) 3 times, yo, (sl 1-K1-psso)
twice, rep from * to last st, K1.
4th row P to end.

Rep 3rd and 4th rows 3 more times. Bind off.

To finish
Press each piece lightly on WS with warm iron, omitting rib pat. Sew down edges of picot hem on the WS of skirt and sleeves.

Smocking
To work the smocking (see Helping Hand) thread the tapestry needle with 2 strands of A. With bodice front lacing, find the center of the raised rib pat. Then working into the first and second K st from outside edge, bring needle through from the WS over the two K sts, and through to the WS. Repeat once more. Repeat across the row, then work into alternate sts above and below to form smocking. Repeat on back bodice and sleeve edges matching the pattern. Using a crochet hook and MC, work 2 rows of single crochet around back neck opening, making 2 buttonhole loops into last row on the left side (see page 161). Sew on buttons to correspond.
Join side and sleeve seams. Sew in sleeves. Sew on ruffle, easing in any fullness to fit to inside of picot hem.

HELPING HAND

Smocking on knitting
Smocking is used as a form of decorative gathering to control the fullness of the fabric. Because of the elasticity in knitted fabrics, they are particularly suitable for smocking. In smocking, two rib stitches are pulled together, so a rib pattern background is required. One knit stitch followed by three or four purl stitches makes a good background.

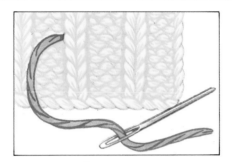

1 *Thread a blunt-ended tapestry needle with one or two strands of contrasting smocking yarn. Join the yarn behind the second knit stitch of the first two ribs to be worked into by neatly running through the loops of the rib. Insert the needle from the back to the front on the left-hand side of the rib stitch and pull yarn through.*

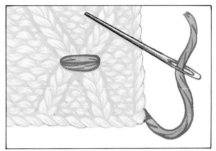

2 *Take the yarn across the front of the knit stitch, the previous purl stitches and the first knit stitch. Insert the needle from the front to back of work and pull the yarn through. Take another back stitch over the same group of stitches and leave the yarn at the back.*

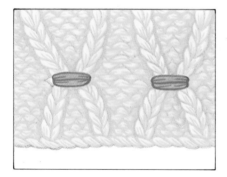

3 *Bring the needle from the back of the work to the front of the work on the left-hand side of the next group of two knit stitches, and draw the yarn through. Smock this group of stitches to the right of the smocking yarn together. Continue in this way to the end of the row.*

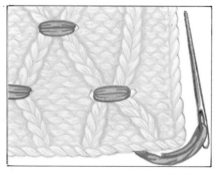

4 *The next row of smocking is worked over alternate stitches about ½ inch above the last row. Work the row as before from right to left, ensuring that the long strand between backstitches is not pulled too tightly.*

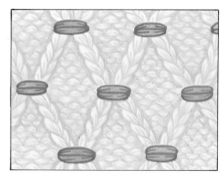

5 *Continue smocking at intervals in this way until the area to be smocked is covered. On the smocked yoke of the dress the first row of smocking is worked across the center of the yoke and then filled in above and below.*

Pleated Skirt

This skirt can easily be adapted to fit a larger or smaller child, by making the skirt width twice the waist measurement. The length can be varied according to the number of the stitches cast on.

Size
To fit 22″ waist
Length 12″

Materials
☐ 2oz of a sport weight yarn in main color MC
☐ 2oz in each of 2 contrasting colors A and B
☐ One pair size 6 knitting needles
☐ 1¼″-wide elastic long enough to fit waist plus ½″ extra

Gauge
20 sts and 32 rows to 4″ over pat using size 6 needles.

To save time, take time to check gauge.

Skirt

Using MC, cast on 60 sts. **Beg
with a K row, work 13 rows in St st.
14th row P1, * yo, P2 tog, rep from
* to last st, P1.
Beg with a K row, work 3 rows in
St st.
18th row Join in A, *K1 tbl, rep
from * to end.
Using A, work first 17 pat rows as
before.
Next row Join in B, *K1 tbl, rep
from * to end.
Rep from ** 5 times more, working
pleats in B, MC and A in turn.

Waistband

Using MC, cast on 102 sts. Beg with
a K row, work 21 rows in St st.
Bind off.

To finish

Pin and press the pleats into place.
With the RS facing each other, sew
skirt and waistband tog.
Insert elastic, fold waistband in
half and sew down loosely.
Join center back seam and
waistband seam.
Fold the last two picot stitches up
for the hem and sew down.

HELPING HAND

Knitted pleats

When working pleats, the skirt is
knit sideways with the cast-on and
bound-off edges meeting at the
back to form the center back seam.
The pleats are held into place
when completed and the hem is
folded to the wrong side when
finishing.
When choosing your yarn,
remember that a pure wool will
hold its pleated shape better than a
synthetic yarn.

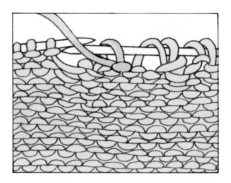

1 *Cast on the required number of stitches. Then beginning with a knit row, work 13 rows in stockinette stitch.*

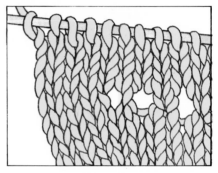

2 *For the 14th row work a picot as instructed. Then beginning with a knit row, work 3 more rows in stockinette stitch.*

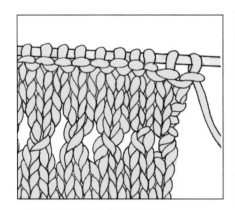

3 *The 18th row is worked by knitting through the back of the loops of all the stitches to the end of the row.*

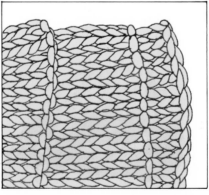

4 *Repeat first to 18th rows for the required length, ending with an 18th row. Bind off. Pin and press the pleats in position folding in each pleat at the picot row and the 18th row.*

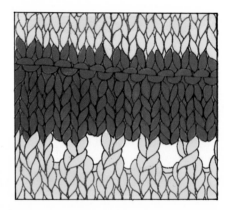

5 *Each pleat could be worked in a different color. Another interesting striped effect can be achieved by working the first to 14th pattern rows in the main color and the 15th to 18th rows in a contrasting color as shown above.*

Diamond Overalls

The sweet striped diamond motifs make these overalls a real gem! Active kids will never want to take them off.

Sizes
To fit 20[22:23]″ chest
Length to waist 17[20:23¼]″
Note Instructions for larger sizes are in brackets [ ]; where there is only one set of figures it applies to all sizes.

Materials
- ☐ 7[7:9]oz of a fingering weight yarn in main color MC
- ☐ 1¾oz in each of 3 contrasting colors A, B and C
- ☐ One pair each of sizes 1 and 3 knitting needles
- ☐ Narrow elastic for back waist
- ☐ 2 buttons (optional)

Gauge
30 sts and 41 rows to 4″ over St st using size 3 needles.

To save time, take time to check gauge.

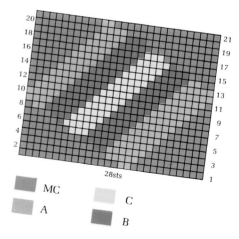

28sts

MC   A   C   B

Diamond Overalls

Right leg

Using smaller needles and MC, cast on 56[60:64] sts. Work in K2, P2 rib for 1½".

Next row Rib 0[1:2], * rib 1, pick up strand between st just worked and next st and work into back of it – called M1 –, rep from * to last 0[1:2] sts, rib to end. 112[118:124] sts.

Change to larger needles and beg with a K row, cont in St st until leg measures 2¾[3½:4¾]" from beg, ending with a P row.

Place motif

Next row K20[23:26] MC, K first row of chart, K to end in MC.

Next row P64[67:70] MC, P 2nd row of chart, P to end in MC.

Keeping chart correct, cont in this way. Work 2 rows, ending with a P row.

Place motif

Next row Work 64[67:70] sts in pat, K first row of chart, work in pat to end.

Next row Work 20[23:26] sts in pat, P 2nd row of chart, work in pat to end.

Cont in this way until motifs are complete, then cont in MC only until leg measures 6[7¾:9¾]" from beg, ending with a P row.

Place motif

Next row K46[49:52] MC, K first row of chart, K to end in MC.

Next row P38[41:44] MC, P 2nd row of chart, P to end in MC.

Cont in this way until chart is complete, then cont in MC only until leg measures 10¾ [12½:14½]" from beg, ending with a P row.

Shape crotch

Bind off 2 sts at beg of next 4 rows. Dec one st at each end of next row and then every other row until 94[100:106] sts rem.

Work even until leg measures 12¼[14¼:16¼]" from beg, ending with a P row.

Place motif

Next row K52[55:58] MC, K first row of chart, K to end in MC.

Next row P14[17:20] MC, P 2nd

row of chart, P to end in MC.

Cont in this way until chart is complete, then cont in MC only until leg measures 14½[16½:18½]" from beg, ending with a P row.

Place motif

Next row K10 [13:16] MC, K first row of chart, K to end in MC.

Next row P56[59:62] MC, P 2nd row of chart, P to end in MC.

Cont in this way until chart is complete, then cont in MC only until leg measures 17[20:23¼]" from beg, ending with a P row.

Shape waist

1st and all RS rows K to end.
2nd row P75[80:85], turn.
4th row P56[60:64], turn.
6th row P37[40:43], turn.
8th row P18[20:22], turn.
10th row P75[80:85], turn and leave rem 19[20:21] sts on a st holder.

Change to smaller needles.

Next row K1, P2[P0:P1], *K2, P2, rep from * to end.

Next row *K2, P2, rep from * to last 3[0:1] sts, K2, P1[K0:K1].

Rep last 2 rows for 2¾", ending with a WS row.

Bind off in rib.

Left leg

Work as for right leg, reversing the position of motifs by reading odd numbered rows of chart as P rows from left to right, and even numbered rows as K rows from right to left and all shapings by reading K for P and P for K throughout.

Bands (make 2)

Using larger needles and MC, cast on 16 sts.

Work in St st until band measures 15[16¼:17]" from beg, ending with a P row.

Bind off.

Bib

Join front seam.

With RS facing and using larger needles and A, K across 19[20:21] sts on left leg st holder, then across

19[20:21] sts on right leg. 38[40:42] sts.

Beg with a P row, cont in St st in stripe pat as foll:
2 rows A, 3 rows B, 3 rows C, 3 rows B, 1 row A.

Rep last 12 rows until bib measures 2½" from beg, ending with a P row

1st buttonhole row Work 4 sts in pat, bind off 3 sts, work 24[26:28] sts in pat, bind off 3 sts, work 4 sts in pat.

2nd buttonhole row Work in pat to end, casting on 3 sts over those bound off in previous row.

Work 4 more rows in stripe pat.

Change to MC and K one row.

Change to smaller needles and cont in rib as foll:

Next row *P2, K2, rep from * to last 2[0:2] sts, P2[0:2].

Next row K2[0:2], *P2, K2, rep from * to end.

Rep last 2 rows for ¾".

Bind off in rib.

Fold waist rib in half.

Sew edges to bib.

Side bib ribs

With RS facing and using larger needles and MC, pick up and K26 sts along side of bib, working between top of waist rib and top edge.

Complete as for first size of top of bib rib.

To finish

Press lightly on WS with warm iron, omitting ribbing.

Join back and leg seams.

Cut elastic to fit back waist and sew an end to each side of bib inside the waist rib. Sew down the rib to encase elastic.

Fold the bands in half lengthwise and join the long edges. Sew bands in position on back waist.

Sew on buttons or pull ends of bands through buttonholes and knot as shown in photo.

The advantages of knot fasteners is that they can be adjusted to give a snug fit to accommodate growing children.

Patch Overalls

Liven up these loose-fitting overalls with boldly colored patches. The bib section is lined with matching fabric to prevent it from dropping and to give a neater finish.

Size
To fit 24-25″ chest
Length from crotch 17¼″

Materials
☐ 9oz of a knitting worsted weight yarn in main colour MC (blue).
☐ Small amounts of black, white, green, red, yellow, pink and purple for patches
☐ One pair each of sizes 3 and 8 knitting needles
☐ ½ yd of 36″-wide blue fabric for lining bib
☐ 18″ of 1″-wide elastic
☐ 2 buttons
☐ Tapestry needle

Gauge
19 sts and 19 rows to 4″ over St st using size 8 needles.

To save time, take time to check gauge.

Right front

Using smaller needles and MC, cast on 28 sts. Work in K1, P1 rib for 3¼".

Inc row * Rib 5, pick up strand between st just worked and next st and work into back of it – called M1 –, rep from * to last 3 sts, rib 3. 33 sts.

Change to larger needles and work in St st until front measures 7¾" from the beg, ending with a WS row.

Next row K5, * M1, K4 rep from * to last 3 sts, K3. 38 sts.

Work even until front measures 10¼" from beg, ending with a WS row.

Next row K4, * M1, K6, rep from * to last 4 sts, K4. 43 sts.

Work even until front measures 18¾" along side seam.**

Shape crotch

Bind off 6 sts at beg of next row, then 3 sts at beg of every other row twice and one st at beg of every other row once.

Work even until front measures 25¼" from beg, ending with a RS row.

Shape bib

Bind off 3 sts at beg of next row, then 2 sts at beg of every other row 4 times. 19 sts.

Work even until front measures 30¾" from beg.

Bind off.

Left front

Work as for right front, reversing shaping.

Left back

Work as for right front to **.

Shape crotch

Bind off 6 sts at beg of next row, then 3 sts at beg of every other row once and 2 sts at beg of every other row once.

Work even until back measures 25¼" from beg, ending with a WS row.

Shape bib

Bind off 3 sts at beg of next row, then 2 sts at beg of every other row until one st rem. Fasten off securely.

Right back

Work as for left back, reversing shaping.

Shoulder straps (make 2)

Using larger needles and MC, cast on 5 sts. Work in St st until strap measures 11" from beg, ending with a WS row.

Buttonhole row K2, yo, sl 1-K1-psso, K1.

Work 5 rows in St st.

Rep buttonhole row.

Work 5 rows in St st. Bind off.

Patches

First patch

Using larger needles and green, cast on 15 sts. Work 21 rows in St st.

Bind off.

2nd patch

Using larger needles and red, cast on 3 sts. P one row.

Cont in St st, inc one st at each end of every row 7 times. 17 sts.

Work even for 15 rows.

Dec one st at each end of every row 7 times. 3 sts.

Bind off.

3rd, 4th and 5th patches

Work as for first patch, but working 3rd patch in yellow with 19 sts and 30 rows, 4th in green with 30 sts and 29 rows and 5th in red with 28 sts and 34 rows.

Embroidery

Foll charts work color patterns on patches, using duplicate stitch (see page 50).

Make 2 small pompons (see page 127), one in white and one in yellow and sew to bunny and end of clown's hat respectively.

Using yellow, work French knots (see page 33) over clown's hat on 2nd patch. Using red, work a French knot for clown's nose and work mouth in satin st (see page 162). Using black, work 2 cross sts for eyes and outline mouth in stem st (see page 78).

Using red, work bunny's eye on 3rd patch with a cross st.

For 4th patch, embroider 3 French knots in each window as flowers and one in center of door, using red.

Work tail on kite of 5th patch, using chain st (see page 163) and black. Using white, work bows at corners of kite in detached chain sts (see page 163) and ties on tail in straight sts.

To finish

Sew front and back seams.

Press all pieces on WS with warm iron.

Sew patches to overalls as desired (see Helping Hand).

Cut out fabric pieces for front and back bibs using knitted pieces as guide and adding a ⅝" seam allowance. Sew side seams of

HELPING HAND

Patching knitted garments

Patches can be decorative as well as practical. Children's garments wear and tear easily, and the patches provide extra padding on the areas most likely to wear first. A selection of patches added at random to a garment can be fun.

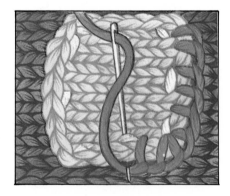

Using a contrasting color, work a patch to the required size. Then pin and baste it in position. Sew the patch to the garment using either an overcast stitch or a blanket stitch as shown above. Do not pull the stitching tightly. Remove basting and press lightly.

fabric pieces. Turn under edges all
around and sew down.
Sew side seams on overalls.
Sew lining to inside of bib.
Sew straps to back and sew 2
buttons to top of bib.
Cut piece of elastic in half and sew
each 9″ piece tog in a circle
overlapping ½″.
Fold ankle rib in half to WS, insert
elastic and sew rib in place.

1st patch

2nd patch

3rd patch

4th patch

5th patch

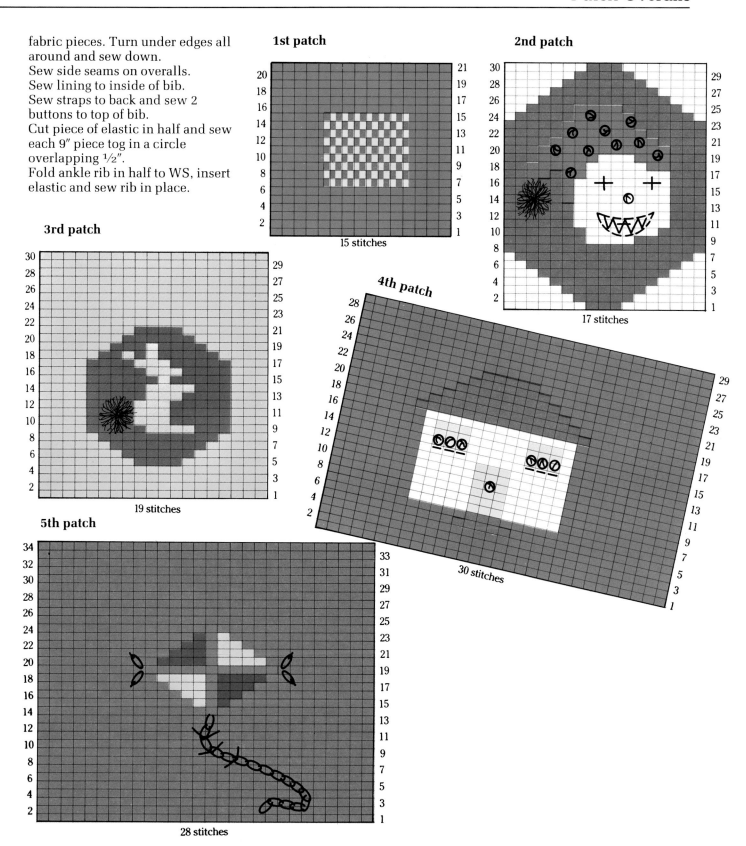

15 stitches

17 stitches

19 stitches

30 stitches

28 stitches

117

Chapter 4
ACCESSORIES

What better way to keep the children cozy and warm on winter days than with knitted accessories made in the colors of your choice.

In the following pages individual patterns for hats, scarves, socks and mitts are given (see pages 126, 128, 130 and 134) to suit ages ranging from 4-8 years old – the scarves, of course, could be lengthened and would be equally ideal for ten year olds. The knitting skills and stitch patterns for these garments are fairly simple to work and could easily be attempted by a newcomer to knitting.

Alternatively, knitters with a little experience may prefer to make the matching set of Penguin Warm-ups, given on the opposite page, or the tricolor Mittens and Socks (see page 123) to keep off the chill of snowy days, and generally add a bright, colorful note to your child's winter wardrobe.

Penguin Warm-ups

Keep your child warm with this adorable collection of perky penguin accessories which are designed to brighten cold snowy days.

Sizes
Scarf: 9″ × 45½″
Hat, socks and mittens: to fit 5[6: 7] year old
Note Instructions for larger sizes are in brackets [ ]; where there is only one set of figures it applies to all sizes.

Materials
Scarf:
☐ 3½oz of a sport weight yarn in main color MC (blue)
☐ 1½oz in contrasting color A (white)
☐ Small amounts in each of 2 contrasting colors B (yellow) and C (black)

Hat:
☐ 1[1:1½]oz of a sport weight yarn in main color MC
☐ 1½oz in contrasting color A
☐ Small amounts in each of 2 contrasting colors B and C

Socks:
☐ 1½[2:3]oz of a sport weight yarn in main color MC
☐ 1oz in contrasting color A
☐ Small amounts in each of 2 contrasting colors B and C

Mittens:
☐ 1½oz of a sport weight yarn in main color MC
☐ 1oz in contrasting color A

All accessories:
☐ One pair each of sizes 3 and 5 knitting needles
☐ Size C crochet hook
☐ Tapestry needle

Gauge
24 sts and 32 rows to 4″ over St st using size 5 needles.

119

Penguin Warm-ups

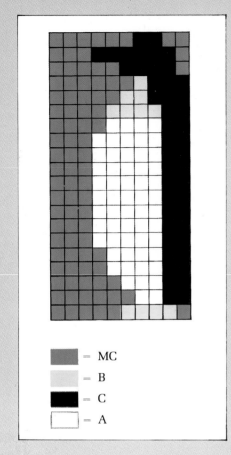

= MC
= B
= C
= A

Scarf

Using smaller needles and MC, cast on 54 sts. Work 8 rows in garter st (K every row).

Change to larger needles and beg with a K row, work 2 rows in St st. Beg working penguin pat as foll:

1st row K3 MC, * 1 MC, 4 B, 5 MC, rep from * to last st, K1 MC.

2nd row P1 MC, * 6 MC, 2 A, 2 C, rep from * to last 3 sts, 3 MC.

3rd row K3 MC, * 2 C, 3 A, 5 MC, rep from * to last to st, K1 MC.

4th row P1 MC, * 4 MC, 4 A, 2 C, rep from * to last 3 sts, 3 MC.

These 4 rows form penguin pat. Cont working from the chart, beg with 5th row, until 20 rows have been completed.

Break off A, B and C.

Work 6 rows in St st, using MC only.

Beg working snowflake pat as foll:

Note When working snowflake pat, use a separate length of yarn for each dot. When changing colors for dots, twist yarns on WS to avoid holes.

1st row K6 MC, * 2 A, 2 MC, rep from * to last 8 sts, 2 A, 6 MC.

2nd row P5 MC, * 4 A, 6 MC, rep from * to last 9 sts, 4 A, 5 MC.

3rd row K5 MC, * 4 A, 6 MC, rep from * to last 9 sts, 4 A, 5 MC.

4th row P6 MC, * 2A, 8 MC, rep from * to last 8 sts, 2 A, 6 MC.

Beg with a K row, work 12 rows in St st, using MC only.

17th row K1 MC, * 2 A, 8 MC, rep from * to last 3 sts, 1 MC, 2 A.

18th row P4 A, * 6 MC, 4 A, rep from * to end.

19th row K4 A, * 6 MC, 4 A, rep from * to end.

20th row P1 MC, * 2 A, 8 MC, rep from * to last 3 sts, 2 A, 1 MC.

Work 12 rows in St st, using MC only.

These 32 rows form the snowflake pat. Rep snowflake pat until scarf measures approx 42" from beg, ending after 6 rows of St st.

Work the penguins in reverse, turning the chart upside down and beg with 20th row, which now becomes first row as foll:

1st row K1 MC, * 6 MC, 2 C, 2 MC, rep from * to last 3 sts, 3 MC.

Cont working from chart until penguins are completed. Work 2 rows in St st, beg with a K row. Change to smaller needles and work 8 rows in garter st.

Bind off.

Hat

Using smaller needles and A, cast on 112[114:116] sts. Work in K1, P1 rib for 3¼[3½:4]"

Change to larger needles and MC and work 2 rows in St st, beg with a K row.

Beg working penguin pat as foll:

1st row K2[3:4] MC, * 4 B, 6 MC, rep from * to last 9[10:11] sts, 4 B, 5[6:7] MC.

Last row sets the penguin pat. Cont working from the chart, beg with 2nd row until 20 rows have been completed.

Break of A, B and C.

Work 2 rows in St st, using MC only.

Beg working snowflake pat as foll:

1st row K6[7:8] MC, * 1 MC, 2 A, 9 MC, rep from *, ending last rep 7[8:9] MC.

2nd row P6[7:8] MC, 4 A, * 8 MC, 4 A, rep from * to last 6[7:8] sts, work in MC to end.

3rd row As first row.

4th row P7[8:9] MC, 2 A, 1 MC, * 9 MC, 2 A, 1 MC, rep from * to last 6[7:8] sts, work in MC to end.

Cont in St st with MC only until hat measures 8¾[9:9¾]″ from beg, ending with a WS row.

Next row K1[0:2], * K3 tog, rep from * to end.

Thread yarn through rem sts, pull tightly and fasten off securely.

Socks

Leg

Using smaller needles and A, cast on 42[44:46] sts. Work in K1, P1 rib for 2[2½:2¾]″.

Change to larger needles and MC and beg with a K row, work 2 rows in St st. Work 20 rows of penguin chart in reverse order, turning the chart up side down and beg with 20th row, which now becomes first row as foll:

1st row K1[1:3] MC, * 5 MC, 2 C, 3 MC, rep from * to last 1[2:3] sts, work in MC to end.

2nd row P1[2:3] MC, * 2 MC, 4 C, 3 MC, rep from * to last 1[2:3] sts, work in MC to end.

Cont working from chart until all 20 rows have been completed. Break off A, B and C.

Work 2 rows in St st, using MC only and dec one st at each end of first row. 40[42:44] sts.

Beg working snowflake pat as foll:

1st row K6[7:8] MC, * 1 MC, 2 A, 9 MC, rep from * once, 1 MC, 2 A, 7[8:9] MC.

2nd row P6[7:8] MC, * 4 A, 8 MC, rep from * once, 4 A, 6[7:8] MC.

3rd row K6[7:8] MC, * 4 A, 8 MC, rep from * once, 4 A, 6[7:8] MC.

4th row P6[7:8] MC, * 1 MC, 2 A, 9 MC, rep from * once, 1 MC, 2 A, 7[8:9] MC.

Using MC only, cont in St st, dec one st at each end of next row and then every 6th row until there are 32[36:40] sts, *and at the same time* beg next snowflake pat on foll 13th row as foll:

1st and 2nd sizes only

Next row K2 tog MC, K9[10] MC, 2 A, 10 MC, 2 A, 9[10] MC, K2 tog MC.

3rd size only

Next row K13 MC, 2 A, 10 MC, 2 A, 13 MC.

All sizes

Complete snowflake pat as before and cont working snowflake motifs every 12 rows alternating as before on rem 32[36:40] sts until sock measures 9½[9¾:10¼]″ from beg, ending with a WS row.

Divide for instep and heel

Next row K8[9:10] MC and sl these sts onto a safety pin, work center 16[18:20] sts in pat, sl last 8[9:10] sts onto a safety pin.

Cont in pat as before until the instep measures 4[4¾:5½]″, ending with a WS row.

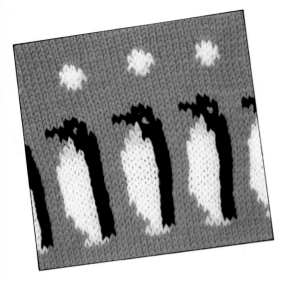

Shape toe
1st row K2, K2 tog tbl, K to last 4 sts, K2 tog, K2.
2nd row P to end.
Rep last 2 rows until 6[8:10] sts rem, ending with a P row.
Bind off.
Shape heel
With RS facing, join yarn at inner edge of last set of sts, K these sts using same needle, K across sts from first safety pin. 16[18:20] sts.
P one row.
Turn heel
1st row Sl 1, K14[16:18] sts, turn.
2nd row Sl 1, P13[15:17] sts, turn.
3rd row Sl 1, K12[13:14] sts, turn.
4th row Sl 1, P11[12:13] sts, turn.
Cont in this way working one st less before turning on every row until the row "sl 1, P3[5:7] sts, turn" has been worked.
Next row Sl 1, K3[5:7] sts, pick up loop between sts and K this loop tog with next st, turn.
Cont in this way, working one more st, before working picked up

loop tog with next st, until the row "sl 1, P14[16:18] sts, P loop tog with next st, turn" has been worked. 16[18:20] sts.
Cont in St st until sole is same length as instep on toe shaping.
Shape toe
Shape as for instep.
Bind off.

Mittens
Using smaller needles and A, cast on 38[40:42] sts. Work in K1, P1 rib for 1½".
Change to larger needles and MC, and beg with a K row, work 2 rows in St st.
Shape thumb gusset
Beg working snowflake pat as foll:
1st row K8[8:9] MC, 2 A, 8[9:9] MC, pick up strand between st just worked and next st and K into back of it – called M1 –, K2 MC, M1, K8[9:9] MC, 2 A, 8[8:9] MC.
2nd row P7[7:8] MC, 4 A, 18[20:20] MC, 4 A, 7[7:8] MC.
3rd row K7[7:8] MC, 4 A, 7[8:8] MC, M1, 4 MC, M1, 7[8:8] MC, 4 A, 7[7:8] MC.
4th row P8[8:9] MC, 2 A, 22[24:24] MC, 2 A, 8[8:9] MC.
5th row K18[19:20] MC, M1, K6, M1, K18[19:20] MC.
Cont in MC only, inc as before until there are 52[54:58] sts.
P one row.
Next row K34[35:38] sts, turn.
Next row P16[16:18] sts, turn.
Work 1¼[1½:1½]" in St st on these 16[16:18] sts, ending with a WS row.
Shape top
Next row K2 tog to end of row. 8[8:9] sts.
P one row.
Next row K0[0:1], * K2 tog, rep from * to end.
Cut yarn, thread through rem sts, pull tightly and fasten off.
Rejoin yarn to base of thumb and K first 18[19:20] sts, pick up and K2 sts from base of thumb and K18[19:20] sts to end. 38[40:42] sts.
P one row.
Beg working snowflake pat as foll:

Next row K12[13:14] MC, 2 A, 10 MC, 2A, 12[13:14] MC.
Next row P11[12:13] MC, 4A, 8 MC, 4 A, 11[12:13] MC.
Next row K11[12:13] MC, 4 A, 8 MC, 4 A, 11[12:13] MC.
Next row P12[13:14] MC, 2 A, 10 MC, 2 A, 12[13:14] MC.
Work 12 rows in St st, using MC.
Beg working snowflake pat as foll:
Next row K6[7:8] MC, *2 A, 10 MC, rep from * once, 2 A, 6[7:8] MC.
Next row P5[6:7] MC, * 4 A, 8 MC, rep from * once, 4 A, 5[7:7] MC.
Next row K5[6:7] MC, * 4A, 8 MC, rep from * once, 5[6:7] MC.
Next row P6[7:8] MC, * 2 A, 10 MC, rep from * once, 2 A, 6[7:8] MC.
Using MC only, cont in St st until mitten measures 2¾[3¼:3½]" from base of thumb, ending with a WS row.

Shape top
1st row * K1, K2 tog, K13[14:15], K2 tog tbl, K1 rep from * to end.
2nd and every other row P to end.
3rd row * K1, K2 tog, K11[12:13], K2 tog tbl, K1, rep from * to end.
5th row *K1, K2 tog, K9[10:11], K2 tog tbl, K1 rep from * to end.
7th row * K1, K2 tog, K7[8:9], K2 tog tbl, K1 rep from * to end.
P one row.
Bind off.

To finish
Using MC, embroider a French knot (see page 33) on each penguin for eyes.
Using crochet hook and MC, work a row of single crochet (see page 161) evenly along each long edge of scarf to prevent curling.
Cut 9" lengths of A for fringe on scarf. Using 3 strands for each fringe, work fringe knots along both ends of scarf (see page 35).
Sew back hat seam. Make pompon (see page 127) and sew on top of head.
Sew toe, back and side seams on socks.
Sew thumb, top and side seams on mittens.

Mittens and Socks

Use up your odds and ends of yarn to knit these tricolor mittens and socks. The instructions are given for one size only but the lengths can be altered where indicated.

Mittens

Using set of four double-pointed needles and A, cast on 42 sts. Sl 14 sts onto each of 3 needles, using the 4th needle to work with. Mark the beg of round with a colored thread.

1st round *K1, P1, rep from * to end.

Rep last round until rib measures 3¼".

Change to MC and work 4 rounds in St st.

Shape thumb

Next round K20, pick up strand between st just worked and next st and K into back of it – called M1 –, K2, M1, K20.

Work even in St st for 3 rounds.

Next round K20, M1, K4, M1, K20. Cont to inc in this way on every 4th row until there are 54 sts, ending with 3 rounds in St st after last inc round.

Divide for thumb

Next round K21, sl next 12 sts onto a st holder and leave for thumb, turn and cast on 2 sts, turn and K21. 44 sts.

Cont in St st until mitten measures 6" from beg or 1" less than desired finished length. (Lengthen or shorten here.)

Shape top

Change to B and shape top as foll:

Dec round K1, sl 1-K1-psso, K16, K2 tog, K2, sl 1-K1-psso, K16, K2 tog, K1.

K next 2 rounds.

Dec round K1, sl 1-K1-psso, K14, K2 tog, K2, sl 1-K1-psso, K14, K2 tog, K1.

K next 2 rounds.

Cont to dec on next round and then

Size

Mittens:
To fit 6-8 year old
Length 6¾"
Width 6¼"
Socks:
To fit 7" foot
Leg length 4"

Materials

☐ 3oz of a fingering weight yarn in main color MC
☐ 1oz in each of 2 contrasting colors A and B
☐ Set of four size 2 double-pointed knitting needles

Gauge

32 sts and 40 rows to 4" over St st using size 2 needles.

To save time, take time to check gauge.

123

on every other row as before until 24 sts rem.

Bind off sts tog or weave these 24 sts tog.

Thumb

With RS facing and using A, K across 12 thumb sts, then pick up and K4 sts from base of cast-on sts. 16 sts.

Cont in St st until thumb measures 1¼" from beg or ¼" less than desired finished length. (Lengthen or shorten here.)

Shape top

Next round K1, * K2 tog, K1, rep from * to end. 11 sts.

Next round K to end.
Next round K1, * K2 tog, rep from * to end. 6 sts.

Break off yarn and thread end through rem sts, pull tightly and fasten off.

Socks

Using set of four double-pointed needles and A, cast on 42 sts. Sl 14 sts onto each of other 3 needles, using the 4th needle to work with. Mark end of round with a colored thread. Work in K1, P1 rib as for mittens for 2½".

Change to MC and work in St st until sock measures 5" from beg or

desired length to beg of heel. (Lengthen or shorten here.) Break off yarn.

Divide for heel

Next row Sl first and last 11 sts of round onto one needle, rejoin yarn and P to end. 22 sts.

Beg with a K row, work 16 rows in St st, ending with a P row.

Turn heel

Next row K14 sts, sl 1-K1-psso, turn.

Next row P7, P2 tog, turn.

Next row K7, sl 1-K1-psso, turn.

Next row P7 sts, P2 tog, turn.

Rep last 2 rows until all sts are on

HELPING HAND

Shaping mittens and socks

A neat smooth finish to the toes of socks and the top of mittens can be achieved by working all the shaping in rounds using a set of four double-pointed needles. By using four needles no uncomfortable seam will be produced. Either "flat" shaping (used for the tricolor mittens and socks) or round shaping can be used for mitten tops and sock toes. If you have never made socks or mittens before, practice the shaping methods before beginning by following these easy steps.

Flat shaping

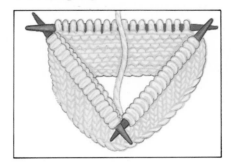

1 *Cast on 48 stitches, slipping 16 of them on each of the three needles. Knit a few rounds on these stitches for the foot or hand section.*

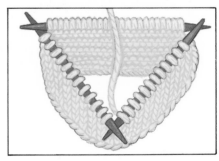

2 *Rearrange the stitches so that half the stitches are divided between the first and third needles. The remaining half of the stitches are placed onto the second needle.*

4 *On the second needle, knit one stitch, slip one stitch, knit one stitch, pass slipped stitch over, continue to knit until three stitches remain, knit next two stitches together then knit the last stitch.*

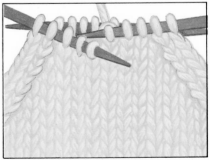

5 *On third needle, knit one, slip one, knit one, pass slipped stitch over, knit to end of needle. Knit one round. Repeat steps 3 to 5 until 20 stitches remain, ending with decrease row.*

one needle.

Next round K4 sts; using 2nd needle, K rem 4 heel sts, pick up and K10 sts down side of heel; using 3rd needle, K across 20 sts of instep; using 4th needle, pick up and K10 sts up other side of heel, then K the first 4 sts onto this needle.

Shape instep

1st round K to end.

2nd round Using first needle, K to last 3 sts, K2 tog, K1; using 2nd needle, K to end; using 3rd needle, K1, sl 1-K1-psso, K to end.

Rep last 2 rounds until 42 sts rem.

Work even until sock measures 4″ from where the sts were picked up at the heel or 1½″ less than desired finished length to end of toe. (Lengthen or shorten here.)

Change to B and K one round.

Shape toe

1st round Using first needle, K to last 3 sts, K2 tog, K1; 2nd needle, K1, sl 1-K1-psso, K to last 3 sts, K2 tog, K1; using 3rd needle, K1, sl 1-K1-psso, K to end.

Work even in St st for 2 rounds.

Rep last 3 rounds until 22 sts rem, then K across sts on first needle.

Bind off sts tog or weave sts tog.

Round shaping

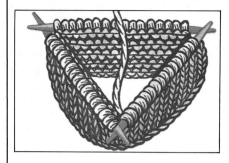

1 Cast on 48 stitches, then divide these stitches onto three needles. Working with the fourth needle, work a few rounds in stockinette stitch.

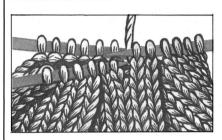

2 On the next round, knit six stitches, knit the next two stitches together, repeat from the beginning of the round until all the stitches have been worked. Knit one round. On the next round, knit five stitches, knit two stitches together, repeat to the end of the round. Continue in this way, working one stitch less before each decrease on each successive repeat, until 12 stitches remain.

3 On the next round knit two stitches together six times. Cut the yarn and thread through remaining stitches, pull tightly and fasten off securely.

Thumb shaping

1 Cast on 18 stitches and divide them equally between the three needles. Work a few rounds. On the next round knit one stitch, knit two stitches together, repeat from the beginning of the round until all the stitches in the round have been worked.

2 On following round, knit two stitches together six times. Cut the yarn, thread through remaining stitches and fasten off securely.

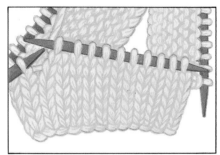

3 Using the first needle, knit to the last three stitches, knit next two stitches together, then knit the last stitch in the normal way.

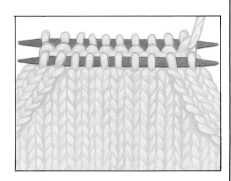

6 Now knit stitches from first needle onto third needle so that all stitches are equally divided between two needles. Graft two sections together neatly and fasten off.

Pompon Hat

Knit this snug hat for a small child in even pastel stripes using four different colors. It has cosy ear flaps and will stay firmly in place with ties under the chin. Top it all off by attaching fluffy pompons.

Size
To fit 4-6 year old.

Materials
- [ ] 1½oz of a fingering weight yarn in main color MC
- [ ] 1oz in each of contrasting colors A, B and C
- [ ] One pair each of sizes 2 and 3 knitting needles
- [ ] Tapestry needle

Gauge
28 sts and 40 rows to 4″ over St st using size 3 needles.

To save time, take time to check gauge.

Main part
Using smaller needles and MC, cast on 119 sts.

1st row K1 * P1, K1, rep from * to end.

2nd row P1 * K1, P1, rep from * to end.

Rep last 2 rows for 1½″ ending with a 2nd row.

Inc row Rib 7, (pick up strand between st just worked and next st and work into back of it – called M1 –, rib 13) 8 times, M1, rib to end. 128 sts.

Change to larger needles and beg with a K row, work in St st and stripe pat as foll:
Work 4 rows MC, 4 rows A, 4 rows B and 4 rows C.
Cont in stripe pat as set, carrying color not in use loosely up side of work and working until hat measures 9″, ending with a WS row.
Shape top
1st row K8, * sl 1-K1-psso, K2 tog, K14, rep from * to last 12 sts, sl 1-K1-psso, K2 tog, K8.
2nd and all WS rows P to end.
3rd row K7, * sl 1-K1-psso, K2 tog, K12, rep from * to last 11 sts, sl 1-K1-psso, K2 tog, K7.
5th row K6, * sl 1-K1-psso, K2 tog, K10, rep from * to last 10 sts, sl 1-K1-psso, K2 tog, K6.
7th row K5, * sl 1-K1-psso, K2 tog, K8, rep from * to last 9 sts, sl 1-K1-psso, K2 tog, K5.
9th row K4, * sl 1-K1-psso, K2 tog, K6, rep from * to last 8 sts, sl 1-K1-psso, K2 tog, K4.
11th row K3, * sl 1-K1-psso, K2 tog, K4, rep from * to last 7 sts, sl 1-K1-psso, K2 tog, K3.
13th row K2, * sl 1-K1-psso, K2 tog, K2, rep from * to last 6 sts, sl 1-K1-psso, K2 tog, K2.
15th row K1, * sl 1-K1-psso, K2 tog, rep from * to last 5 sts, sl 1-K1-psso, K2 tog, K1.
16th row * P2 tog, rep from * to end.
Break off yarn, thread end through rem sts and pull tightly. Fasten off.

Ear flaps and ties
Using smaller needles and MC, cast on 5 sts.
1st row K2, P1, K2.
2nd row P2, K1, P2.
Rep until tie measures 10¼″.
Next row K1, inc in next st, P1, inc in next st, K1.
Next row P1, inc in next st, P1, K1, P1, inc in next st, P1.
Cont in rib, inc one st at each end of every row, one st in from edge until there are 43 sts.
Work even in rib for 8 rows.

Bind off.

To finish
Sew hat seam, reversing seam for brim.
Sew flaps inside hat to last row of brim rib.
Make 3 pompons (see below).
and sew one to top of hat and one to each tie.

HELPING HAND

Making pompons
For a fuller, denser pompon increase the size of the central hole on the cardboard templates so that more yarn can be wound around.

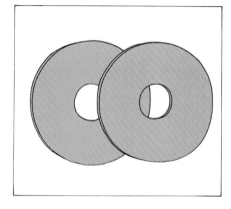

1 Cut two circles of thin cardboard the size required for the finished pompon. Cut a smaller circle from the center of both pieces.

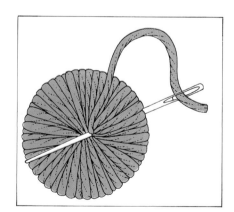

2 Wind the yarn evenly around both thicknesses of card in the same direction until the hole is full. It may be easier to thread the yarn through the holes using a tapestry needle.

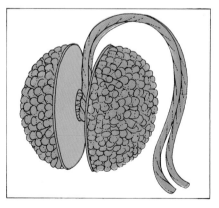

3 Cut the yarn around the outer edge, slipping blade of scissors between two circles. Take a long length of yarn and tie securely around the center between the two circles. Remove the cardboard, and fluff out the pompon. Trim if necessary.

Ribbed Scarf

Make this warm winter scarf in fisherman's rib stitch. Then add fringe or tassels to give it a flare.

Materials
☐ 7oz of a knitting worsted weight yarn
☐ One pair of size 8 knitting needles

Gauge
12 sts and 16 rows to 4″ over fisherman's rib pat using size 8 needles.

To save time, take time to check gauge.

To make
Cast on 42 sts. Beg fisherman's rib pat as foll:
1st row K to end.
2nd row Sl 1, *K1, K into st below next stitch on left-hand needle, rep from * to last st, K1.
The last row forms the fisherman's rib pat and is rep throughout. Cont in pat until scarf measures 80″ from beg or desired length.
Next row K to end.
Bind off very loosely.

To finish
Do not press.
Add fringe or tassels at each end as desired (see Helping Hand).

Give the scarf a sporty look by knotting both ends.

HELPING HAND

Fisherman's rib

Fisherman's rib pattern produces a very dense fabric. It has a lot of give and is especially good for scarves and shawls. Because of its density, it is warmer than ordinary ribbing.

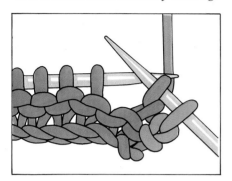 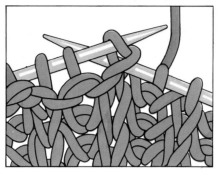 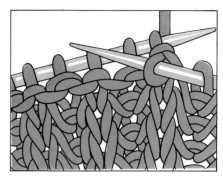

1 *Once the cast-on row has been worked with an even number of stitches, knit one row. Then beg the next row. Slip the first st and knit the second stitch.*

2 *Insert the tip of the right-hand needle into the stitch below the next stitch on the left-hand needle from the front of the stitch through to the back, making sure the needle also passes through the center of the stitch above.*

3 *Wrap the yarn around the needle and draw a loop through. Slip the top stitch and the stitch knit into off the needle at the same time. Knit the next stitch. Repeat steps 2 and 3 to end of row.*

Tassels

Tassels lend an attractive finishing touch to scarf ends. Make them in matching or contrasting colors, or a mixture of both. Between 5"-6" is a popular length.

1 *Cut a piece of cardboard to the required length and width of the tassel. Wind the yarn evenly around the cardboard.*

2 *Thread a blunt-ended needle with a matching yarn, insert it under all the wound strands and knot securely.*

3 *Cut through all the strands of the yarn at the untied edge and remove the piece of card. Trim ends.*

Fair Isle Socks

Worked in a classic Fair Isle pattern these attractive socks are a welcome addition to any wardrobe. They can be worn over the top of ankle length corduroy or denim trousers.

Size
To fit 6 to 8 year old
Note If desired, adjust lengths where indicated in pattern instructions.

Materials
- □ 1¾oz of a knitting worsted weight yarn in main color MC (blue)
- □ 1¾oz in contrasting color A (green)
- □ Small amounts in 3 contrasting colors B (yellow), C (red) and D (brown)
  One set of four size 6 double-pointed knitting needles

Gauge
22 sts and 28 rows to 4″ over St st using size 6 needles.

To save time, take time to check gauge.

To make
Using MC, cast on 54 sts. Sl 18 sts onto each of 3 needles, using 4th needle to work with. Work in K2, P2 rib for 9 rounds.
Work 2 rounds in St st.
Cont in St st, foll chart for Fair Isle pat and working all 34 rounds of chart. (Lengthen or shorten here.)
At end of last round, break off yarn.

Divide for heel
Sl first 11 sts and last 11 sts of round onto an empty needle for heel and work on these sts only.
Divide rem 32 sts evenly over 2 needles and hold for instep.
With RS facing, rejoin yarn to 22 sts of heel. Working back and forth in rows and beg with a K row, work 16 rows in St st; end with a P row.

Turn heel
Next row K14, sl 1-K1-psso, turn, leave 6 sts unworked at end of row.
Next row P7, P2 tog, turn and leave 6 sts unworked at each end.
Next row K7, sl 1-K1-psso, turn.
Next row P7, P2 tog, turn.
Rep last 2 rows 5 times.
All heel sts are on one needle.
Cont to work in rounds once more.
Next round Using first needle, K across 8 sts of heel, then onto same needle pick up and K10 sts evenly along straight row ends of first side of heel, making 18 sts; K across 16 sts on next needle, then using same needle, K across 16 sts on foll needle, making 32 instep sts; pick up and K10 sts evenly along straight row ends of 2nd side of heel, then using same needle, K across first 4 sts on first needle, making 14 sts. 60 sts.

Shape instep
Rounds now start in center of heel.

K one round.
Next round K to last 3 sts on first needle, K2 tog, K1; K across 32 sts on instep on 2nd needle; then working across 3rd needle, K1, sl 1-K1-psso, K to end.
Rep last 2 rounds 5 times.
Next round K5, K2 tog, K1, K next 10 sts of 2nd needle onto first needle; K12 sts on 2nd needle; using 3rd needle pick off last 10 sts of 2nd needle, K11, sl 1-K1-psso, K5. 46 sts.
Work even in St st until sock measures 1½″ less than desired finished length to end of toe.

Shape toe
Next round K5, K2 tog, K10 on first needle; K all 12 sts on 2nd needle; K10, sl 1-K1-psso, K5 on 3rd needle.
Next round K5, K2 tog, K9 on first needle; K12 on 2nd needle; K9, sl 1-K1-psso, K5 on 3rd needle.
Next round K5, K2 tog, K8 on first needle; K12 on 2nd needle; K8, sl 1-K1-psso, K5 on 3rd needle.
Cont in this way, dec one st on first and 3rd needles for five more rounds, with 6 sts rem on first and 3rd needle and 12 on 2nd.
Next round K6 sts on first needle, K2 sts off 2nd needle (8 sts on first needle); K8 on 2nd needle, pass last 2 sts onto 3rd needle; K8 sts on 3rd needle.
Next round K2 tog at beg and end of every needle until 2 sts rem on each needle.
Bind off.

To finish
Weave in any loose ends.
Press lightly on WS with warm iron.

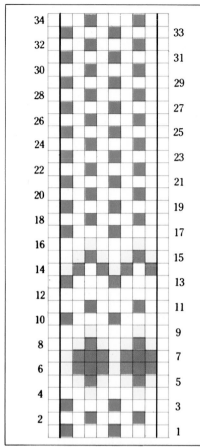

HELPING HAND

Shaping heels

There are several methods of shaping or "turning" a heel, but one of the easiest is the Dutch heel. It is worked in rounds using a set of four double-pointed needles and is seamless. The heel shape is broad and comfortable and the finished heel looks particularly neat. The heel is worked in stockinette stitch, but the remainder of the sock can be worked in any stitch or

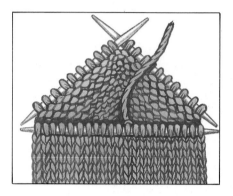

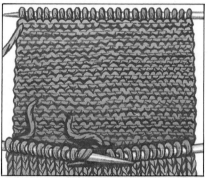

1 To experiment with turning a heel cast on 42 stitches and slip 14 stitches onto each of three needles. Work several rounds, then break off the yarn. Slip the first and last 11 stitches of the round onto an empty needle for a heel. Work on these stitches only. Divide the remaining 20 stitches evenly over two needles and hold this for the instep.

2 With the right side facing, rejoin yarn to the 22 stitches of heel. Beginning with a knit row and working back and forth in rows, work 16 rows in stockinette stitch, so ending with a purl row.

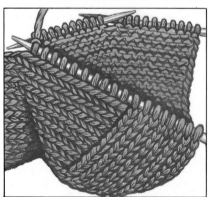

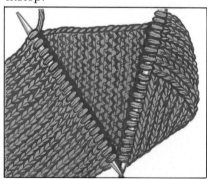

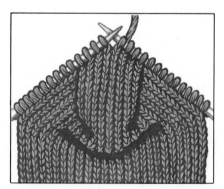

6 Continue to work in rounds once more. With empty needle (first needle), knit across the eight stitches of the heel. Using the same needle, pick up and knit 10 stitches evenly along straight edge of first side of the heel, making a total of 18 stitches.

7 Using the next empty needle (2nd needle), knit across the 10 stitches on the next needle. Using same needle, knit across 10 stitches of the following needle, making a total of 20 stitches. These stitches are for the instep.

8 Using the next empty needle (3rd needle), pick up and knit 10 stitches evenly along straight edge of second side of the heel. Using the same needle, knit across first four stitches on the first needle, making a total of 14 stitches. Work in rounds on these 48 stitches from the center of the heel.

pattern. The back of the heel is worked first by re-sectioning the stitches and working back and forth in rows for a straight section. This section is then shaped to form the base of the heel. The heel and instep stitches are worked together again, working decreases near the instep on the first few rounds. Even to an experienced knitter turning a heel can be quite a challenge, but a great deal of satisfaction can be achieved from knitting the first pair of socks.

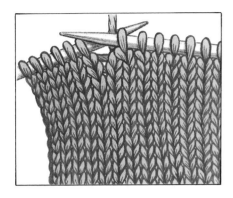

3 *To turn the heel work the first row by knitting 14 stitches, slip one stitch, knit one stitch, pass the slipped stitch over, turn the work around. Leave the six stitches unworked at the end of the row on the needle.*

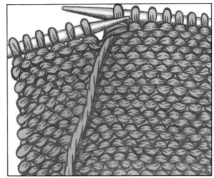

4 *The next row is worked by purling seven stitches, purl next two stitches together in the usual way, turn the work. Leave the six stitches unworked at each end on the needle.*

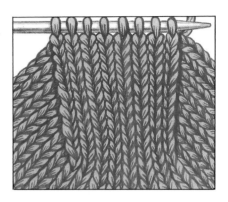

5 *For the next row, knit seven stitches, slip one stitch, knit one stitch, pass the slipped stitch over, and turn the work. On purl row, work seven stitches, purl the next two stitches together and turn. Repeat the last two rows five times more. All the heel stitches are now on the needles.*

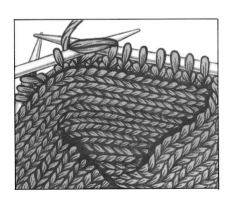

9 *Knit the first round. On the next round, knit to the last three stitches on the first needle, knit next two stitches together, then knit the last stitch in the ordinary way.*

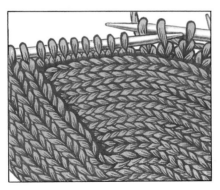

10 *Knit across all the 20 stitches of the instep on the second needle. On the third needle, knit one stitch, slip one stitch, knit one stitch, pass slipped stitch over. Now knit to the end of the needle.*

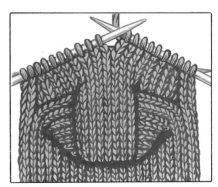

11 *Repeat steps 9 and 10 three times. There are 40 stitches now on the needles. This completes the heel shaping. The sock is then continued without shaping until the toe shaping is reached.*

Clown Scarf

Here's a striped scarf worked in a rib pattern and begun and ended by a glove puppet. The clown faces are embroidered in duplicate stitch.

Size
Length including pompons 47″
Width 7½″

Materials
☐ 1½oz of a knitting worsted weight yarn in each of 4 contrasting colors A (red), B (yellow), C (blue) and D (green)
☐ 1oz in contrasting color E (orange)
☐ One pair size 6 knitting needles
☐ Size C crochet hook

Gauge
24 sts and 34 rows to 4″ over pat using size 6 needles.

To save time, take time to check gauge.

To make
Using A, cast on 46 sts. Beg at first puppet hat and work as foll:
1st row Sl 1, K4, P4, K28, P4, K5.
2nd row Sl 1, P4, K4, P28, K4, P4, K1.
Rep last 2 rows 9 times more.
First puppet face
Change to D and rep last 2 rows 17 times more.
Main part of scarf
Change to B and beg scarf rib pat as foll:
**1st row Sl 1, *K4, P4, rep from * to last 5 sts, K5.
2nd row Sl 1, *P4, K4, rep from * to last 5 sts, P4, K1.
Rep 1st-2nd rows for scarf rib pat.
Cont in pat working in stripes of 34 rows each in B, C, A, D, B, C, A and D.
2nd puppet face
Change to B and beg pat as foll:
Next row Sl 1, K4, P4, K28, P4, K5.
Next row Sl 1, P4, K4, P28, K4, P4, K1.
Rep last 2 rows 16 times more.
2nd puppet
Change to C and rep last 2 rows 10 times more.
Bind off.
Neck ruffles (make 2)
1st row With RS facing and with top of hat toward you and using A, pick up and K46 sts along lower edge of face.
2nd row Sl 1, P to last st, K1.
3rd row Sl 1, *K2, inc into next st, rep from * to end. 61 sts.
4th row As 2nd row.
5th row Sl 1, K to end.
6th row As 2nd row.
Break off A and join in D.
7th to 10th rows As 3rd to 6th rows. 81 sts.

Break off D and join in B.
11th row Sl 1, *K2, inc into next st, rep from * to last 2 sts, K2. 107 sts.
12th-14th rows As 4th-6th rows.
Break off B and join in C.
15th row Sl 1, *K2, inc into next st, rep from * to last st, K1. 142 sts.
16th-18th row As 4th-6th rows.
Bind off.

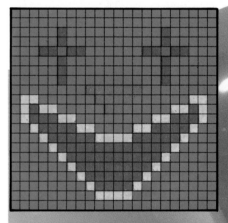

To finish

Using duplicate st (see page 50). embroider features onto faces foll charts.

For hair cut 36 lengths of yarn each 4″ long in assorted colors.

Fold 3 strands tog to form a loop. Using crochet hook, draw loop through work at side of face close to hat, then draw ends through loop and pull to secure knot.

Work 3 fringes at each side of both faces.

Join neck ruffles and back of each head and hat.

Thread a length of yarn through top of hats, pull to gather and secure.

Using E, make 2 pompons and sew one to the top of each hat.

Chapter 5
KNOW~HOW

The equipment and materials needed for knitting are minimal. You can begin simply with a pattern, yarn and needles.

Once you have mastered the basic skills of casting on and binding off (see pages 138-39) and knitting and purling (see pages 140-41) you will easily progress through simple shaping working increasing and decreasing stitches (see pages 145-47) to produce garments you'll be proud to own.

Useful guidance is given for more advanced techniques such as knitting in rounds and colorwork (see pages 150 and 152) with plenty of professional tips for seaming and pressing the finished garment. There are also lots of special finishes given, including making buttons and applying button bands, and a variety of embroidery stitches to prettify the plainest of patterns.

Basic Techniques

CHOOSING YARN

Before beginning any of the knitting projects in the book, take special care when selecting your yarn. Only a generic description of the yarn is given for each pattern. This leaves you scope to choose from the large range of yarns available today and alleviates the problem of trying to find a specific brand name which may not be easily available in your area.

If you are an experienced knitter you will know that the key to selecting yarn is in the gauge given in the pattern. And for those of you who are less familiar with yarn weights – take heart! Choosing the correct yarn is not as daunting as it may seem.

Most yarns give a recommended stitch gauge and needle size on the label. Look for a yarn which recommends the same number of stockinette stitches per 4″ as the gauge in your pattern or as near as possible to the same number. The needle size need not be the same as your pattern specifies, because needle size can be altered. Only when the gauge is given over a lace or textured stitch should you use the recommended needle size as a guide.

If you are still not confident about your choice of yarn, purchase only one ball or skein and test your gauge before buying all you need. Keep two things in mind when making your final decision on your yarn purchase. Firstly stick to the type of yarn specified in the pattern. In other words if the pattern calls for a smooth yarn, then choose a smooth yarn or if it calls for a bouclé, choose a bouclé. Secondly, remember that the amounts given in the instructions are approximate. As with *all*

knitting projects, it is best to find a yarn in a shop or store nearby that will willingly take back your unused skeins. Then you can take one or two balls extra just in case.

GAUGE

All knitting pattern instructions specify a "gauge", which is the number of stitches and rows to a given measurement. You must exactly match the gauge stated or your knitting will not be the same shape or size as the original.

It is very important to check your gauge before beginning a garment. Make a sample square using your chosen yarn and the needle size specified in the pattern. Work the swatch at least 5″ by 5″ and knit the stitch pattern given in the gauge section.

Check with the finishing

No amount of knitting skill can improve on badly selected yarn, so take your time when looking at yarns and you will be rewarded with a lovely finished garment.

instructions and treat the sample as the finished piece of knitting, blocking and pressing if necessary, without stretching it in any way. Allow the swatch to "rest" for ten minutes after it has been blocked or pressed before measuring.

Change the needle size and knit another sample if the first gauge is incorrect. If there are too few stitches, try a smaller needle; likewise, if there are too many stitches, use a larger needle. The size of the needle is not important, the main point is to achieve the required gauge.

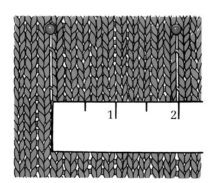

1 *To measure the number of stitches place the tape measure across the knitting and, using pins, mark off 2″ in the center of the swatch. Carefully count the stitches, including any half stitches. Once multiplied across the width of the garment, they can alter the size. If the gauge is given over 4″, count stitches over 4″.*

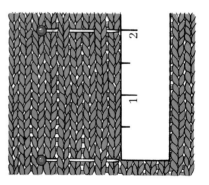

2 *To measure the number of rows, place the tape measure vertically on the swatch. Using pins, mark off 2″ or 4″ and count the rows between. It is easier to count from the bottom of the knitting and work upward. Count carefully as any mistakes could dramatically alter raglan armholes and sleeve shapings.*

CASTING ON

To begin knitting, stitches must first be "cast" onto a needle. There are several ways of casting on stitches. The end results are similar, but the methods are quite different. Usually the choice of method is left to the knitter and only on the odd occasion will a pattern state which one to use. The following instructions show you two popular methods. The first uses two knitting needles and is called the "cable" method. It produces a strong but elastic edge and is widely used for thicker yarns. The second method is called the "thumb" method. It uses only one needle with the thumb of the left hand acting as the second needle. It produces a finer, more elastic edge, suitable for lace knits and baby wear. Practice these two and see which you prefer.

More important than the choice of method is to achieve a neat edge with stitches that are not too tight. If you do cast on tightly it may be advisable to use a larger needle size than the one recommended for working the ribbing.

Cable method

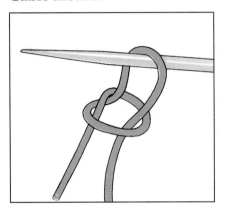

1 Make a slip loop about 4" from the end of the yarn and place it on the needle. Pull the short end to tighten the stitch. Hold this needle in your left hand.

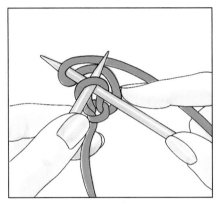

2 Insert the right-hand needle into the loop so that it rests under the left-hand needle in a crossed position. Take the yarn under and over the point of the right-hand needle.

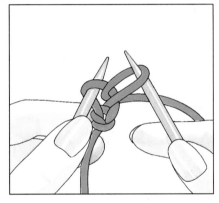

3 With the right-hand needle draw the yarn through the stitch on the left-hand needle to make a new stitch on the right-hand needle. Work loosely on these stitches.

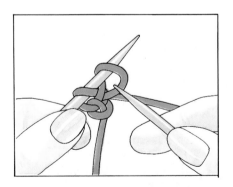

4 Transfer the stitch on the right-hand needle onto the left-hand needle. Always make sure each loop is facing the same direction otherwise the edge will look uneven.

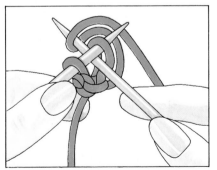

5 Insert the right-hand needle between the two stitches on the left-hand needle, from front to back. Take the yarn under and over the point of the right-hand needle.

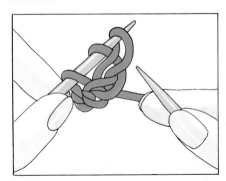

6 Draw the yarn through between the stitches to make a new stitch. Repeat steps 4 to 6 until you have the necessary number of stitches.

Thumb method

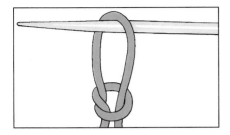
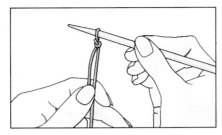
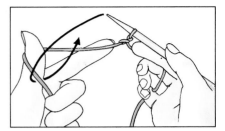

1 *Allowing approximately ¾" of medium yarn for each stitch to be cast on, make a slip loop that distance from the end of the yarn.*

2 *Place the loop on the needle and pull the shorter end to tighten the stitch.*

3 *Hold the needle and the yarn from the ball in the right hand. Wind the shorter end around the thumb of the left hand.*

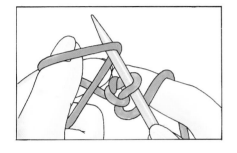
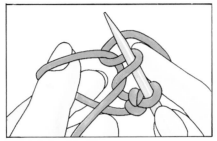
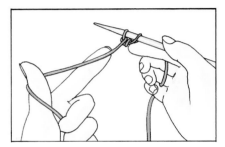

4 *Insert needle through the loop on the thumb, holding this taut in your left hand with the thumb at least 1" away from the needle.*

5 *Take the yarn from the ball under and over the point of the needle and draw it through the loop on the thumb to make a stitch.*

6 *Slip the loop off the thumb. Pull the shorter end to tighten the stitch. Repeat steps 2 to 6 until you have enough stitches.*

HOLDING YARN AND NEEDLES

The correct way to hold the yarn and needles is the one which is the most comfortable and which produces a neat, even knitted fabric.

The yarn is wound around one finger and then over and under the remaining fingers in order to control the flow of the yarn. Right-handed knitters hold the yarn in the right hand and also the needle containing the stitches which have been knitted. The left hand holds the stitches to be knitted. These positions are reversed for left-handed knitters. If you are a beginner, practice the yarn and needle positions given here until you choose the one you like best.

1 *One way to hold the yarn is to wind it completely around the little finger and then over and under the remaining three fingers.*

2 *Alternatively, begin with the little finger and wind the yarn under and over three fingers and loop it around the first.*

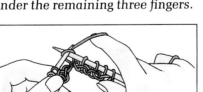

3 *One needle position is where the hands hold the needles over the top with the thumb at the front and the fingers at the back.*

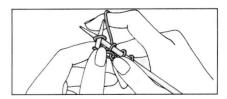

4 *Here the right-hand needle rests at the base of the thumb and first finger and the hand slides forward as each stitch is knitted.*

BASIC STITCHES

There are only two basic stitches in knitting – the knit stitch and the purl stitch. Even the most complicated pattern is made from a combination of only these two stitches. Once these simple techniques are mastered, the knitting possibilities become unlimited.

When every stitch on every row is knitted the fabric is called garter stitch. It is often used for hems and borders because the edges lie flat. When every right-side row is knitted and every wrong-side row is purled and the two are worked alternately the fabric is called stockinette stitch. The right side is smooth and the wrong side is ridged. This is probably the most common of all the patterns. When every right-side row is purled and every wrong-side row is knitted the fabric is called reverse stockinette stitch. Here the right side is ridged and the wrong side is smooth. This is often used for a bouclé or similar yarn as it brings out more texture in the finished garment.

Knit stitch

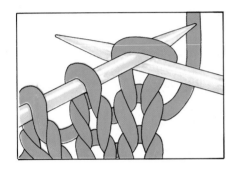
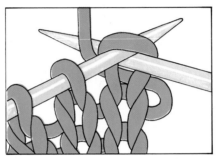
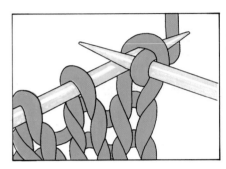

1 Take the needle holding the stitches in your left hand and the empty needle in your right hand. Insert the right-hand needle from right to left through the front of the first knit stitch.

2 With the yarn at the back of the work, and using your index finger, take the yarn under and over the point of the right-hand needle.

3 Draw the yarn on the right-hand needle through the stitch on the left-hand needle.

Purl stitch

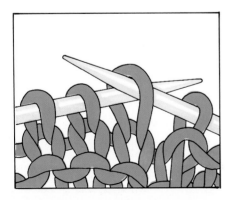
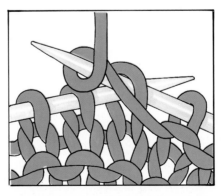
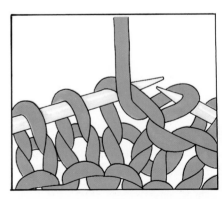

1 Take the needle holding the stitches in your left hand and the empty needle in your right, keeping the yarn at the front of the work.

2 Insert point of right-hand needle from right to left through the front of the first stitch. Take yarn over and under point of right-hand needle.

3 Draw yarn on right-hand needle through the stitch on the left-hand needle, from back through to front, leaving yarn at front.

RIBBING

Ribbing is made from a combination of knit and purl stitches worked alternatively. It produces an elastic fabric which is used mainly for borders, waistbands, cuffs and neckbands to help keep the garment in shape.

When one stitch is knitted and one stitch purled, this is called a single or plain rib. Usually an even number of stitches are cast on for plain rib.

Where two stitches are knitted and two stitches purled, this is called a double rib. It is not as elastic as plain rib and is used mostly for bulkier garments. A number of stitches divisible by four are cast on.

Another popular rib is fisherman's rib (see page 129). It produces a very bold and dense fabric and is especially suitable for menswear. Only the knit stitch is used for fisherman's rib.

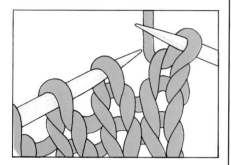

4 Slip the stitch off the left-hand needle, thus completing the knit stitch. Repeat steps 1 to 4 for every stitch.

Single rib

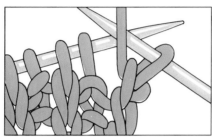

1 Once the cast-on row has been worked, knit the first stitch on the left-hand needle. When this stitch has been worked, and is on the right-hand needle, bring the yarn to the front of the work.

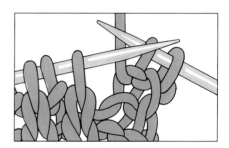

2 Purl the second stitch on the left-hand needle. Transfer to right-hand needle, bring the yarn to the back of the work, ready to knit the next stitch. These two steps are repeated throughout.

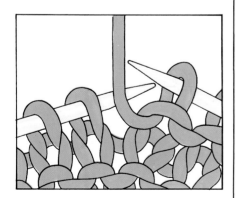

4 Slip the stitch off the left-hand needle onto the right-hand needle, thus completing the purl stitch. Repeat steps 1 to 4 for every stitch.

Double rib

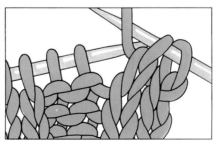

1 Once the cast-on row has been worked, the first two stitches of the row are knitted. When these stitches are on the right-hand needle, bring the yarn to the front of the work.

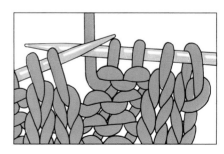

2 The next two stitches on the left-hand needle are purled. When these two stitches have been worked, take the yarn to the back of the work ready for the next stitch to be knitted.

BINDING OFF

At the end of each piece of knitting it is usually necessary to bind off the remaining stitches. This secures them and prevents them from unraveling.

When binding off, care must be taken to keep the edge loose, otherwise the work will be distorted and the stitches could break if the knitting is pulled. This is most important on a neckband which will be stretched every time the garment is worn. The best way to ensure that the edge remains loose is to work the bound-off row using one size larger needle. The following steps show how to bind off on a knit row, but often it will be necessary to bind off on a purl row. To do this, keep the yarn at the front of the work and purl each stitch instead of knitting it. If instructions tell you to bind off in rib or in pattern, follow the steps below, but knit or purl each stitch to keep to the specified pattern.

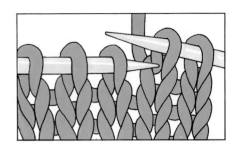

1 *To bind off knitwise keep the yarn at the back of the work. Knit the first two stitches on the left-hand needle in the usual way, working them fairly loosely.*

PICKING UP DROPPED STITCHES

Even the most experienced knitter drops stitches. But do not ignore them or your garment will unravel. On a stockinette stitch fabric, for example, where a single stitch has been dropped down one row, it can easily be picked up using knitting needles.

Where a stitch has formed a run down the knitting, use a crochet hook to pick up the stitches. For garter stitch, turn the work with each picked up stitch.

Stockinette stitch

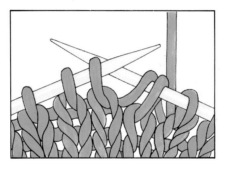

1 *On a knit row, insert the right-hand needle through the dropped stitch from front to back and under the strand of yarn.*

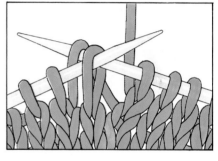

2 *Insert the point of the left-hand needle through the dropped stitch from back to front and lift the stitch over the strand of yarn. Replace the stitch on the left-hand needle. Continue to knit the row.*

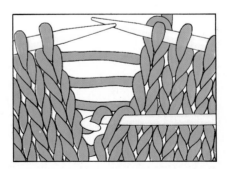

6 *No matter which row you were working on, turn the work so the knit side is facing. Insert the crochet hook through the dropped stitch, from the front to back and under the first strand.*

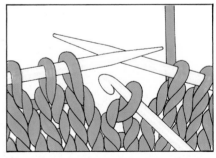

7 *Draw the strand through the stitch. Continue in this way to the top of the ladder, taking care to work up the strands in the correct order. Replace the stitch on the left-hand needle and continue.*

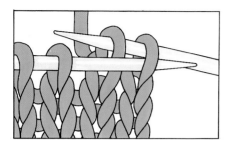

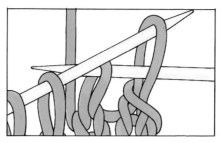

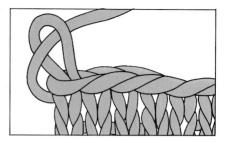

2 Insert the point of the left-hand needle through the front of the first stitch knitted and lift it over the second stitch knitted, then off the needle. One stitch has been bound off.

3 Knit the next stitch on the left-hand needle in the usual way. Lift the second stitch knitted over it and off the needle. Two stitches have now been bound off.

4 Repeat step 3 until only one stitch remains on the right-hand needle. Cut the yarn leaving at least 4" and thread the end through the remaining stitch. Pull end to tighten the stitch.

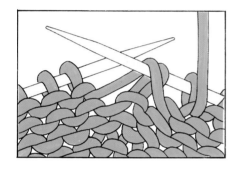

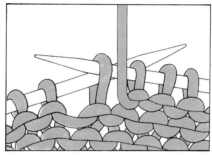

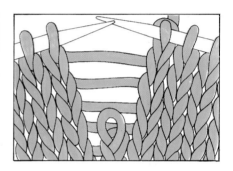

3 On a purl row insert the right-hand needle through the dropped stitch from back to front and then under the strand of yarn.

4 Lift the stitch over the strand of yarn, then transfer the stitch to the left-hand needle and continue to purl in the usual way.

5 Where a stitch has dropped down several rows forming a run, use a crochet hook to pick up the stitch. Firstly slide the stitches away from the needle points.

Garter stitch

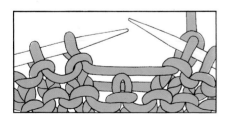

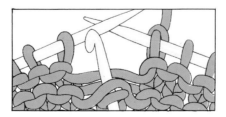

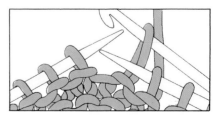

1 On a garter stitch fabric the method is a little more complicated. Turn the work for each stitch you pick up so that the first strand lies behind the dropped stitch, rather than in front of it.

2 Insert the crochet hook from the front to back through the stitch and under the first strand. Draw the strand through the dropped stitch.

3 Turn the work and carefully remove the crochet hook. Work from step 1, making sure the strand lies behind the dropped stitch. Continue in this way to the top of the run. Replace stitch on the appropriate needle and continue

JOINING IN NEW YARNS

It is easier to join in new balls of yarn at the selvage, so that when the garment is finished the ends can be sewn into the seam. This is easier than having to weave the ends into the knitting itself. The quantity of yarn needed to complete a row is roughly four times the row length.
To avoid wastage if the yarn is very limited or expensive, joins can be made in the middle of the row by splicing. Another occasion when yarn may be joined in the middle of the row is when changing color. A method is shown for joining in a new color. It is neat and safely secures a new yarn in pattern where the old color will be used again in the same row.

Splicing

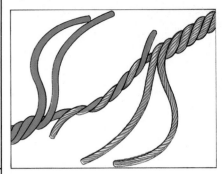

Unravel about 3" of both old and new yarns. Retwist the ends together to make one strand. To secure spliced yarns once they have been twisted, rub the spliced section quickly between the flat of the palms of the hands. Gently tug at the splice and if it feels as if it might pull apart, dampen the join and repeat the rubbing process. Continue knitting, taking extra care over the stitches which follow the splice.
Once the spliced yarn has been knitted any unevenness will disappear.

Joining at the selvage

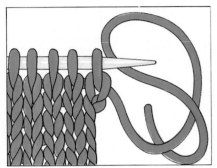

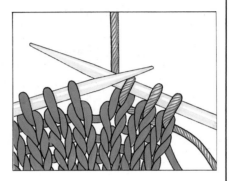

1 When the remaining length of yarn is insufficient to complete a row, leave a length to sew in at the edge of work. The recommended length is approximately 6".

2 Start knitting with a new ball also leaving a length. With slippery yarns, like chenille and silk, knot the ends together loosely. Untie before sewing into a seam.

Adding a new color

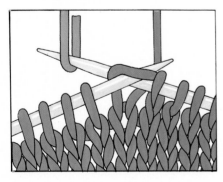

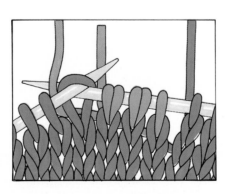

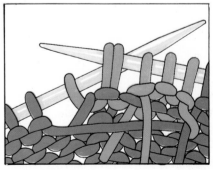

1 Insert the right-hand needle into the next stitch on the left-hand needle. Leaving the old yarn at the back of the work, wind the new yarn around the right-hand needle, leaving this end at the back.

2 Knit the next stitch in the ordinary way with one thread of the new yarn, then knit the next two stitches with the yarn doubled. Leave the short end and continue with the new yarn as required.

3 The old yarn may be used again in the same row, but do not pull too tightly across the back of work. On the next row, work the two threads as one stitch in the usual way.

INCREASING AND DECREASING

It is often necessary to increase the width of the knitting on the needles. There are various ways of doing this depending on the stitch pattern and how many stitches are required. Here we show three methods: the bar increase, making a stitch and a lifted increase.

The bar increase is used when a pattern reads "increase one stitch" usually abbreviated as "inc one st" or "knit into the front and back of the next stitch". This method of increasing can be worked into any stitch of the row.

Stitches sometimes have to be added all along a row. Once a rib has been completed, for instance, a mass increase is often necessary. These increases can be worked into the knit stitch with bar increases or they can be made more invisibly by "making a stitch".

The increase called "make one" is worked by picking up the bar before the next stitch on the left-hand needle. This can be worked on a purl row as well as a knit row, and is abbreviated in patterns as "M1".

Some methods of increasing are more visible, and are intended to produce decorative effects. An example of this is the "knit one below" method also called the "lifted increase". For this a stitch is picked up from the previous row and worked into at the same time as the new row. Both stitches should be worked quite tightly to prevent a hole being produced.

On most knitting patterns it will be necessary to reduce the width of the knitting, for example on neck shaping or at the top of a sleeve. As with increasing there are several ways of decreasing and below we show the simplest method – knitting two stitches together, abbreviated as "K2 tog". This decrease can be worked in any position on a row. A mass decrease is worked by decreasing into each pair of stitches across the row, and is used, for example, at the top of a hat.

Increases and decreases are not only used for shaping. They can also be worked in unison to create decorative stitch patterns such as eyelets.

Bar increase

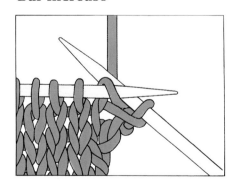

1 Insert the right-hand needle knitwise into the front of the stitch on the left-hand needle and knit the stitch in the usual way, but do not slip the stitch off the left-hand needle.

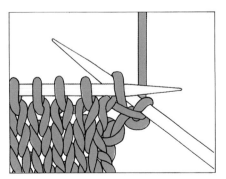

2 Insert the right-hand needle knitwise into the same stitch, through the back of the loop this time, and knit this stitch.

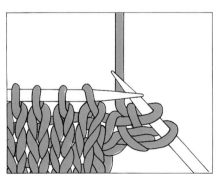

3 Slip the stitch off the left-hand needle. You have now made two stitches from one stitch.

Making a stitch knitwise

  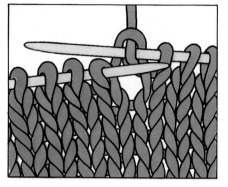

1 With the right side of the work facing, knit to the position where a new stitch is needed in the row.

2 With the right-hand needle, pick up the strand that lies between the stitch just worked and the next stitch on the left-hand needle by inserting the needle from front to back under the strand. Then slip it onto the left-hand needle by inserting the left-hand needle from front to back under the strand.

3 Knit the strand in the usual way. This produces an increase which is visible and creates a hole. Where an invisible increase is needed, the new loop is knit into the back to cross it. Repeat these three steps until the required number of stitches are on the needles. On the following row purl into all of the new stitches in the usual way.

Making a stitch purlwise

1 With the wrong side of the work facing, purl to the position where a new stitch has to be made.

2 With the right-hand needle, pick up the strand between the stitch just worked and the next stitch on the left-hand needle by inserting the needle from front to back under the strand. Do not stretch the yarn. Then slip it onto the left-hand needle by inserting the left-hand needle from front to back under the strand.

3 Purl the strand in the usual way. This produces a visible increase and creates a hole. Where an invisible increase is needed, the new loop is purled into the back to cross it. Repeat these three steps until the required number of stitches have been worked.

Lifted increase knitwise

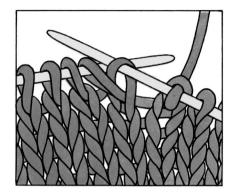  

1 With the right side of the work facing, insert the right-hand needle into the stitch below the next stitch on the left-hand needle from the front through to the back of the loop, being careful not to insert the needle through the stitch above.

2 Knit the stitch in the usual way by taking the yarn under and over the point of the right-hand needle and drawing it through the stitch.

3 Then knit the stitch above the lifted stitch in the usual way. Repeat from step 2 until the required number of stitches are on the needle. On the following row, purl into all of the new stitches in the usual way.

Lifted increase purlwise

1 With the wrong side of the work facing, insert the right-hand needle into the stitch below the next stitch on the left-hand needle, this time from the back through to the front of the loop and being careful not to insert the needle through the stitch above.

2 Purl the stitch in the usual way by taking the yarn over then under the point of the right-hand needle and drawing it through the stitch. Purl the next stitch in the usual way. Continue to increase until the required number of stitches are on the needles.

Knitting two together

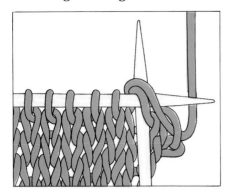 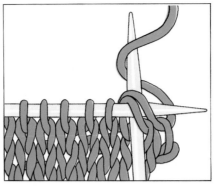 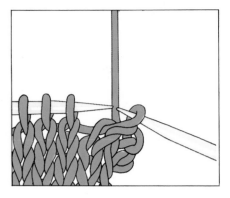

1 Insert the right-hand needle knitwise through the second stitch, then the first stitch on the left-hand needle at the same time.

2 Take the yarn under and over the point of the right-hand needle and draw the yarn through both the first and second stitches.

3 Drop the first and second stitches off the left-hand needle, thus decreasing one stitch.

EYELETS

Eyelets provide the simplest way of making a small buttonhole, to use on a delicate garment such as a baby's, or form the basis of many interesting patterns, from dainty openwork designs to more elaborate lace patterns. They are an excellent way of producing a broderie Anglaise type of knitted fabric, or a decorative edging to carry ribbons or ties.

The principle involved in making an eyelet is quite simple, as it consists of making a stitch by taking the yarn over the right-hand needle and working the next two stitches together. Eyelets may be placed close together on a row. Work at least two rows between each pattern to separate them, otherwise they can blend together forming a different type of fabric.

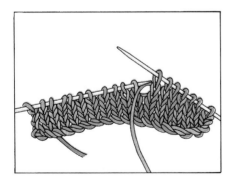 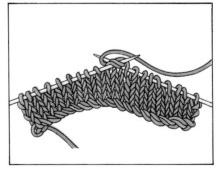 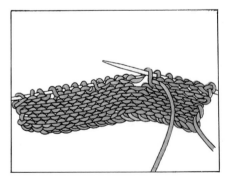

1 Work at least four rows in stockinette stitch before making an eyelet row. With the right side of the work facing, knit to the position where the eyelet hole is to be placed. Bring the yarn from the back of the work to the front of the work between the two needles.

2 Then take the yarn over the top of the right-hand needle to the back of the work and knit the next two stitches together in the usual way. A new loop is created on the right-hand needle. Knit to the position where the next eyelet is to be placed and repeat the whole process again as from step 1.

3 On the following row, purl to the new loop which was made on the previous row and purl into it, thus making a small hole. Purl each stitch and new loop to the end of the row. Work at least two rows before making the next eyelet row.

SLIPPING STITCHES

When a stitch is passed from one needle to the next without being knitted, it is called "slipping" a stitch. Pattern instructions abbreviate it as "sl". When the stitch is slipped onto the next needle, it pulls the stitches either side of this stitch together and produces a stronger fabric. Often the stitches at each end of every knit row are slipped. This makes a neat strong edge and is a good selvage. When sewing the seams, it is easy to pick up the alternate slipped stitches on the seams. On raglan shaping and neckbands, a stitch is often slipped in the border to make the edge strong.

Stitches are slipped for many lacy patterns. On cable patterns, stitches are slipped onto a cable needle and held at the front or back of the work until they are required. A stitch can also be slipped from a striped row to produce a Fair Isle effect without having to strand the yarn across the back of the work.

Slipping knitwise

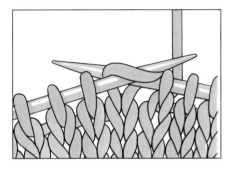 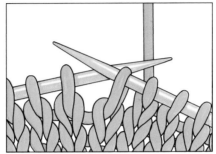

1 *To slip a stitch knitwise, insert the point of the right-hand needle through the next stitch on the left-hand needle, from the front of the loop through to the back. Leave the yarn at back of the work.*

2 *Without wrapping the yarn around the needle, slip the stitch off the left-hand needle onto the right-hand needle. When working decreases with a slip stitch, the knit stitch is slipped knitwise in this way.*

Slipping purlwise

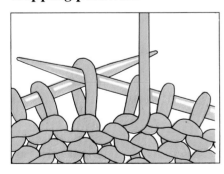 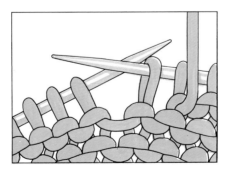

1 *To slip a stitch purlwise, insert the point of the right-hand needle through the next stitch on the left-hand needle from the front of the loop.*

2 *Slip the stitch onto the right-hand needle, holding the yarn in front of the work gently. If the next stitch is to be purled, keep the yarn at the front. In slipstitch color patterns both knit and purl stitches are usually slipped purlwise.*

KNITTING IN ROUNDS

To knit a round a set of four needles or one circular needle is used. This produces a seamless tubular fabric, which is ideal for socks, skirts and the body section of pullovers.

A circular needle consists of two short needles, joined together by a lightweight flexible nylon strip. Both circular and double-pointed needles are available in a similar range of sizes as ordinary needles.

Too few stitches on a circular needle will stretch the work out of shape, so it is essential to obtain the correct length of circular for the piece you are knitting. Narrow tubes, for example sleeves and gloves, must be worked on sets of four double-pointed needles as circular needles do not come short enough for them. There are, however, circular needles short enough for neckbands and turtlenecks.

When knitting in rounds, the right side of the fabric is always facing, as the work is not turned at the end of the row. The wrong side of the fabric will form on the inside of the tube. To work in stockinette stitch every round must be knitted, therefore in reverse stockinette stitch every round is purled. To work in garter stitch, the first round is knitted, the second round is purled, and these two rounds are repeated to the required length. Ribbing is worked as if working on straight needles. Make sure a knit stitch always lies above a knit stitch and a purl stitch above a purl. It is very important to mark the beginning of the round with a small piece of thread, because it is not easily visible in the actual knitting. As one round is completed, slip the thread onto the right-hand needle to keep it between the last stitch and the first stitch of every round.

Knitting on four needles

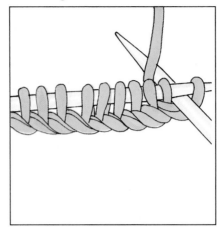

1 *Cast on using a pair of ordinary knitting needles the same size as the set of double-pointed needles to be used.*

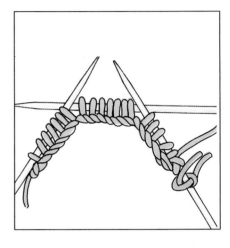

2 *Divide the stitches evenly onto three double-pointed needles. Place a colored marker on the needle before the first stitch in the round.*

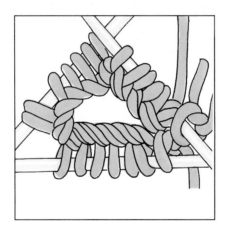

3 *Arrange the three needles to form a triangle. Make sure that none of the stitches are twisted, as this can cause an uneven edge. This is the most difficult step to learn when knitting with four needles as it feels very awkward to try to hold three needles and to keep the stitches from twisting at the same time. But you will soon learn the knack.*

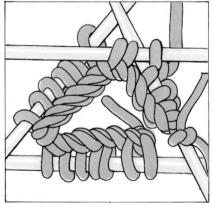

4 *Use the fourth needle to knit the stitches off the other needles. Working the first stitch quite tightly, work across all three needles until the end of the round is completed. Move the marker to the beginning of the next round and continue to knit with the spare needle. Repeat steps 4 and 5 as long as instructed in the pattern. You will find that you will need to work all stitches reasonably tightly or the needles will slip out. After knitting a few rounds you will develop a smooth way of working, keeping an even tension.*

Circular needles

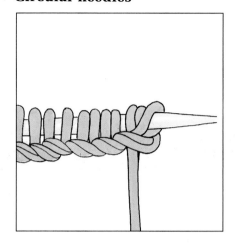

1 Using a pair of ordinary knitting needles the same size as the circular needle, cast on the required number of stitches using the desired cast-on method.

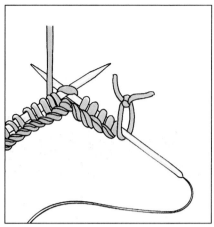

2 Knit these stitches from the ordinary needle onto the circular needle easing them onto the flexible part of the needle as the solid area becomes full. With a contrasting color make a looped marker and slip it onto the circular needle to mark beginning of round.

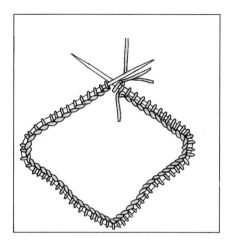

3 Place the knitting on a flat surface and make sure the stitches are not twisted. The right side should be facing you.

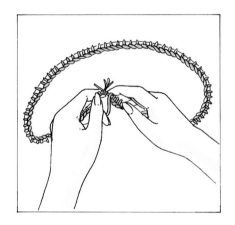

4 Bring the points of the needles together. Slip the marker onto the right-hand needle. Then insert the right-hand needle through the first stitch on the left-hand needle and knit it tightly. This will join the end of the first row to the beginning of the next row.

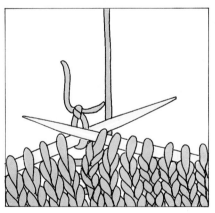

5 Work in the usual way to the end of the round. Continue working each round in the same way, always slipping the colored marker off the left-hand needle and onto the right-hand at the beginning of each round.

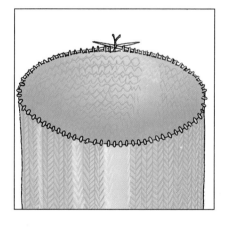

6 Continue working in rounds until the work reaches the required length, remembering to move the marker on each round. Bind off fairly loosely, in the usual way. When working a pullover in this way, once the armholes are reached the tubular fabric is split into equal sections for the back and front. The back and front are then worked in rows to the neckline ready to be finished as instructed in the pattern.

COLORWORK

Colorwork patterns are often called "Fair Isle" after the traditional and world famous colored knitting from the Fair Isles off the northern coast of Scotland.

Many families in the Fair Isles had their own collection of knitting patterns which were used to decorate garments. The patterns range from the very simple to the most intricate and have established symbols, such as stars, anchors, flowers and many geometric designs. The more traditional Shetland items were knitted in natural colors, nowadays the color choice is endless.

Whether you are using traditional patterns or your own designs, working with many colors is a good way of using up leftover yarn. If you have never knitted any colorwork patterns before, try not to work more than two colors in one row when practicing the techniques. You will also find it helpful to make a graph pattern with the colors clearly blocked in, as shown in the small charts on this page. Either use colored pencils or symbols. If planning to use a repeat motif, simply plot out the one block and work from that. For more complicated patterns it is best to draw up the complete design, row by row.

There are two basic methods for working with two or more colors across a row. If the colors are each worked over only a few stitches each, the yarn is stranded across the back. If the colors are worked over more than five stitches the weaving technique is used.

Stranding

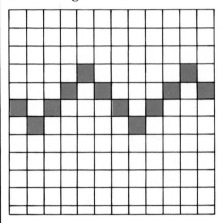

1 *For small regular patterns using two colors only, the color not in use is stranded across the back of the work. This is a more economical method of working with colors as less wool is required and it is slightly quicker to do. Remember that blocking the finished colorwork garment will help to ease out any minor inconsistencies in tension.*

Reading color charts

Charts are often used to simplify knitting instructions. If the chart was written in full it could be very confusing to follow. One square across represents one stitch and one square up represents a new row.

Color patterns are especially suitable for charts. Colors on the charts will either be represented by the actual color to be used or by symbols, so always read the key to the chart. If need be, color in all the appropriate squares, using colored pencils. This may make the chart easier to follow as reading the symbols can be a strain on the eyes. When working from a chart read all the knit rows from right to left and all the purl rows from left to right. If the chart rows have not been numbered, mark all the knit rows on the right-hand edge, and all the purl rows on the left-hand edge. Begin reading the chart from the bottom upward just in the same direction you are knitting the garment. To keep your place on the chart, place it on a flat surface and lay a ruler under the row you are working. As each row is completed make a tick next to the row and move the ruler up one row.

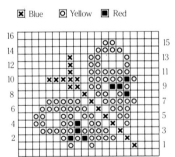

If written out, the first row of the chart above (read from right to left if it is a knit row) would read as follows:

K3 MC, K1 blue, K5 MC, K1 yellow, K2 MC, K1 yellow, K7 MC.

5 *Once the pattern has been completed, check that all the yarns run across the back of the work evenly. If the stranded lengths are pulled too tightly, it will cause the work to pucker. Only practice will improve your colorwork knitting when you will be able to achieve an even fabric.*

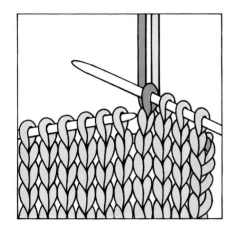

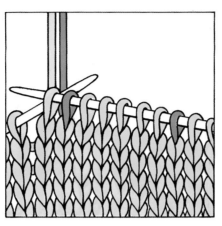

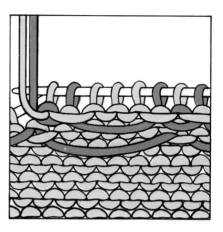

2 *Join in the contrasting color at the beginning of the row. With both yarns at the back of the work, knit to the position where contrasting color is needed. Drop the main color at the back of the work, then pick up the contrasting color. Knit the next stitch using the contrasting color and when the stitch is complete, drop the contrasting color at the back of the work.*

3 *Pick up the main color and knit the next stitch, leaving the contrasting color at the back of the work. Work both colored stitches at the same tension. Continue working in the main color to the position of the next contrasting stitch. Work in this way stranding the yarns loosely across the back of the work.*

4 *On the purl row work in exactly the same way as the knit row, following the chart from the opposite direction. But on the purl row the yarn is held at the front of the work.*

Weaving

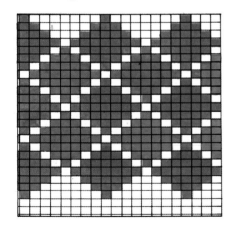

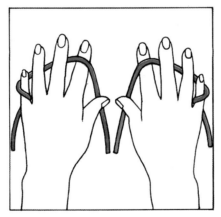

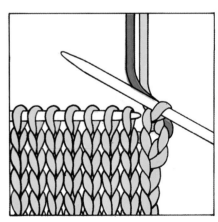

1 *When working a large pattern repeat with more than two colors, use the weaving method. It may be a good idea to wind the contrasting colors onto bobbins to stop them from tangling around one another.*

2 *Thread both the right hand and the left hand with the two colors to be used. Wind the yarn around the little finger and through the remaining fingers, leaving the index finger free to work with.*

3 *Knit the first stitch using the main color and at the same time, with the left hand bring the first contrasting color over the top of the first stitch.*

153

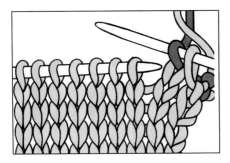

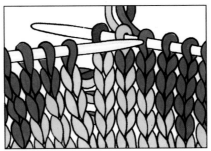

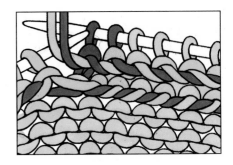

4 *Knit the second stitch in the first contrasting color. This time bring the main color over the top of the second stitch from the right hand.*

5 *Continue to weave the main color while working the first contrasting color. When working a new color, weave the first and main color across back of work.*

6 *On the purl row, work in exactly the same way as the knit row, weaving the yarns at the front of the work. In this way, long loose strands or "floats" are avoided.*

INTARSIA

Many knitting patterns involve working in large blocks of several different colors – sometimes called "intarsia". Geometric and abstract designs are often worked in large blocks of color in this way.
The stranding or weaving techniques, previously mentioned would not be practical for this type of knitting because each color is not used across the entire row but only in an isolated area. It would not be practical to carry the colors back and forth across the back of the work to areas where they are not even needed. Instead a separate ball of yarn can be used for each block of color and the yarn twisted together where they meet.
If the blocks of colors are not large enough to require a ball of yarn, small bobbins of yarn can be used instead. Bobbins are made in strong cardboard with notches cut at the top and bottom. The yarn is wound around the cardboard until it is full. When a row is worked, the bobbins are held at the back of the work and the yarns are twisted when changing colors to avoid a hole. To prevent several bobbins from becoming entangled when not in use, hang them on very short lengths of yarn, and unwind as required.

Making a bobbin

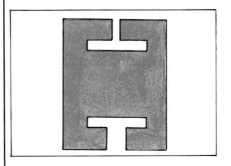

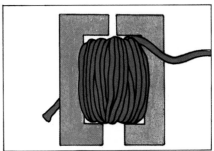

1 *Draw a bobbin shape on a strong piece of cardboard. Using a sharp pair of scissors, cut it out.*

2 *Wind the yarn around the bobbin evenly and in the same direction until the bobbin is full.*

Twisting colours

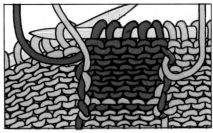

1 *Knit to the position of the contrasting block. Then, twist both yarns together, by taking the main color over the contrast color. Knit the next stitch pulling it tightly to avoid a hole. Work to end of block: change back to main color.*

2 *On the following row, work up to the contrast colored panel, twist the yarns as before, and complete the panel. Then change back to the main color, again twisting the yarns together to avoid making a hole.*

Finishing

BLOCKING AND PRESSING

Correct blocking and pressing, followed by careful sewing up, is the only sure way of producing a well-finished knitted garment. Blocking involves pinning out the knitted pieces to the correct shape and size. Slightly over-large pieces can be eased down and pieces on the small side can be stretched a little to give a correct final measurement. Ribbing should not be blocked or it will lose its elasticity. Therefore, pin around the inner edge of all neckbands and waistbands.

Before pressing it is essential to check the care instructions on the yarn label. Most yarn manufacturers now give a guide on the label in internationally recognized symbols. Both washing and pressing temperatures will be indicated. Before blocking or pressing you should also consider the characteristic texture of a stitch. Both cable patterns and garter stitch will be spoiled by heavy pressing. For the same reason, they should never be ironed on the right side.

Pressing tips
Wool Use a warm iron over a damp cloth.
Synthetics Use a cool iron over a dry cloth.
Cotton and silks Press lightly with a hot iron over a wet cloth.
Mohair and angora Use a hot iron and wet cloth to steam above the fabric on the right side.
Chenille and Lurex Do not iron. Try to avoid dry cleaning as it often takes the bounce out of garments.

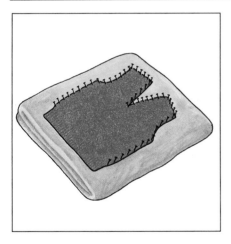

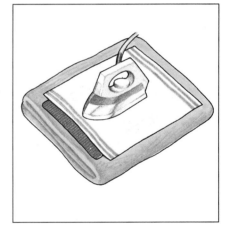

1 Place the garment piece right side down on a springy, padded surface covered with an ironing sheet. A blanket folded and covered with an ordinary clean bed sheet makes a good surface. Pin the piece out to the given measurements. Then pin all around the shape at 1/2" intervals. Take great care to keep the stitches and the rows in a straight line. Check all dimensions to be sure they agree with the pattern size instructions for ease of sewing together – and a good fit.

2 Following the yarn label symbols, place a dry cloth or damp cloth, according to the type of yarn, over the work. If the yarn should not be pressed, leave a damp cloth over the work overnight until completely dry. Keep the work away from direct heat and sunlight to avoid possible shrinkage or fading.

3 If the yarn can be pressed, hold the iron gently over the cloth. It is the heat and the steam created by the iron on the cloth which evens out the knitting, not heavy pressure. Do not use a smoothing action, simply lay the iron on the work lightly and lift off. Continue in this way over all the sections of the garment.

SEAMS

A poor quality seam can spoil the best piece of knitting. Finishing the knitted garment needs a lot of care and attention. Instructions sometimes specify the type of stitch to be used for the seams.

A flat stitch is almost invisible. It is used to give a neat and flat finish on stockinette stitch, garter stitch and on many ribbed sections, such as waistbands. It can be used wherever the shaping has not given an irregular edge to the work.

A backstitch seam gives a firm seam. It is used when joining curved edges such as armholes, or where the seam is sewn across the direction of the knitted stitches as on shaped shoulders.

Another commonly used stitch is the invisible seam. A stitch is picked up from each piece of the work on the right side alternately.

This can be used on garter stitch and stockinette stitch fabrics for side and sleeve seams.

Use a blunt-ended tapestry needle with a large eye when working all types of seams. The blunted end will slip between the knitted stitches without splitting them, and the large eye will carry the yarn through the work easily. Use the original yarn to stitch the seams where possible. Very thick yarns, bouclé, mohair and many fancy yarns are difficult to sew with, so use a finer, smooth yarn in a matching color where necessary.

Flat seam

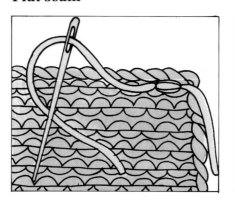

1 *Place the two pieces of the work together with the right sides of work facing each other. Match the pattern stitch for stitch and row for row. Join in the yarn to the right-hand side of one of the completed pieces taking a neat back stitch to make it really secure.*

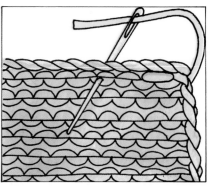

2 *Insert the needle through the edge stitches of both pieces from back to front. Pull the yarn through making sure it is secure.*

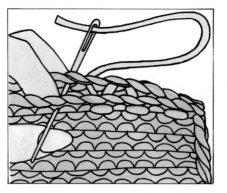

3 *Work back through the next stitch on both pieces. Continue in this way until the seam is complete. Keep the stitches evenly spaced and not too taut.*

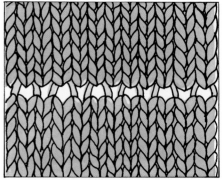

4 *Press the seam so that the inside edge lies flat for a neat finish to the work.*

Backstitch seam

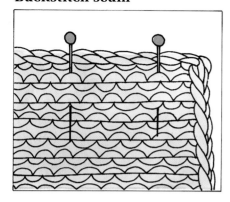
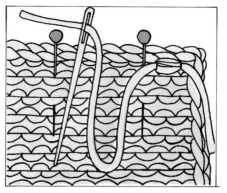
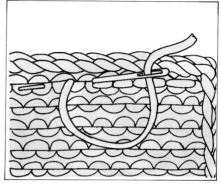

1 *Pin the pieces together with the right sides facing, so that you can work on the wrong side.*

2 *Secure the yarn with two running stitches. Move the needle one knitted stitch to the left at the back of the work and pull the yarn through to the front.*

3 *Re-insert the needle back through where the last stitch was worked. Continue in this way until the seam is complete.*

Invisible seam

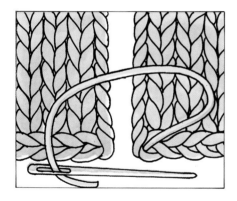
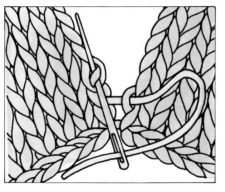

1 *Place the two pieces of the work side by side with the right side of the work facing. Secure the yarn on the wrong side at the lower edge of one piece, then bring the needle through to the right side.*

2 *Take the needle over to the other piece, picking up the center bar of the first stitch. Pull the yarn through tightly, making sure it is secure and the two edges neatly aligned.*

3 *Pass the needle back to the first side and pick up the corresponding stitch. Pull yarn through. Continue in this way. Pull each stitch tightly so it is invisible on the right side of the work.*

PICKING UP STITCHES

It is necessary to pick up stitches for neckbands, collars and armbands. The stitches must be picked up neatly and evenly, and knit with the correct tension otherwise it can spoil the appearance of the garment. Where possible it is easier to work neckbands on two needles, working back and forth in rows. However, it is sometimes necessary to use a circular needle or a set of double-pointed needles to work in continuous rounds.

Be prepared to experiment and if you are not satisfied with the way in which the stitches have been picked up, start again if necessary. Inserting the needle through the center of the stitches, rather than between the stitches, may produce a neater edge. Where shapings have been worked at the edge of the knitted fabric, extra care should be

Finishing

taken to ensure that the pick up row is neat. It may help to knit the first row after picking up the stitches. This forms a ridge on the right side of the work which partly covers the picked up stitches to disguise any irregularity.
When you are working in a different color to that used for the main pieces, a neater result can be obtained by picking up the stitches in the main color; change to the contrast color after the pick up row.

Picking up the neckband

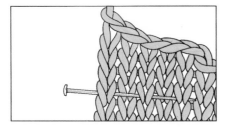

1 When picking up stitches for a neckband, begin by dividing it into equal sections using pins. Calculate how many stitches must be picked up from each section.

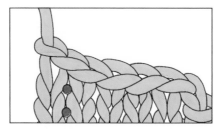

2 Pick up the stitches one complete stitch in from the edge of the work.

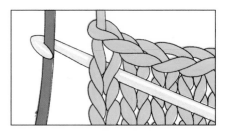

3 It may be easier to pick up the stitches with a crochet hook. Begin at the right-hand edge and, with right side of work facing, insert hook through the first row, one stitch in from the edge. Wind yarn under and over the hook.

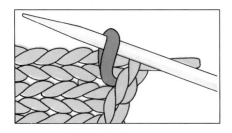

4 Draw the yarn through the first stitch to the right side of work to make a stitch and slip it onto the knitting needle.

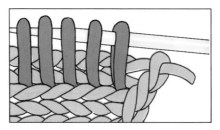

5 Continue in this way, picking up about three stitches for every four row ends.

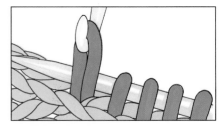

6 Pull each stitch through with the hook and then transfer it to the needle. When the center front neck is reached, the stitches are knit from the stitch holder. If they have been bound off one st is picked up for every stitch bound off; as is the back neck.

BUTTONHOLES

The most common fastening for knitted garments is the button and buttonhole. This can be made quite easily in a number of ways. The method used to make the buttonhole will largely depend on the weight and texture of the fabric, and the size and position of the button to be used.
Sweaters, cardigans and jackets usually feature horizontal buttonholes. There is a reinforced version for outdoor, heavyweight garments.
Vertical buttonholes are more likely to pull apart, and are best kept for more decorative positions where they are not under any strain, such as on flaps of pockets. Fine lacy designs and baby garments only require tiny buttonholes. These are produced by the eyelet method and are the simplest to work.

Vertical buttonhole

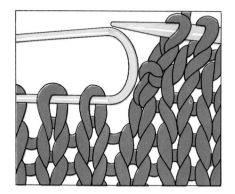 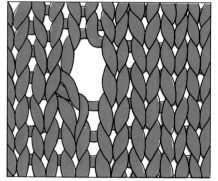

1 Vertical buttonholes are made by dividing the work to form a split. Knit along the row to the position of the buttonhole and turn. Leave remaining stitches on a stitch holder. Continue on this set of stitches up one side of buttonhole for the required depth, ending at the split edge. Slip the edge stitches on alternate rows for a neat finish. Do not break off the yarn at this point because you will need to use it again in step 2.

2 Join in a new ball of yarn to work up the second side of buttonhole. Knit one row less than the first side, ending at the split edge. Break off the yarn. Take up yarn from first side and work across last set of stitches. Weave in the loose ends securely.

Eyelet buttonhole

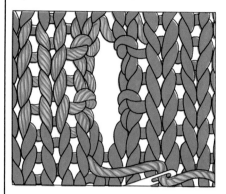

Eyelet buttonholes are worked over one row. Knit along the row to the position of the buttonhole. Bring the yarn to the front of work to make a yarn over. Knit the next two stitches on left hand needle together. On the next row purl the yarn over. A small, neat hole is formed by the yarn over. Because this type is not strengthened by cast-on and bound-off stitches, it is only suitable for delicate buttons.

Horizontal buttonhole

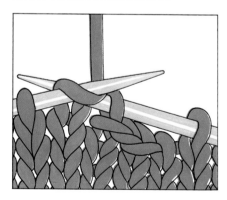 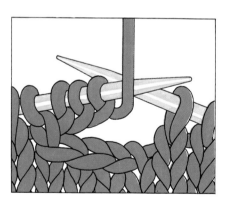 

1 Horizontal buttonholes are worked over two rows. Knit along the row to the position of the buttonhole. Bind off a number stitches appropriate to the button size (usually two or three) and continue knitting to the end of the row.

2 Knit along the next row to the position of the buttonhole. Cast on stitches to replace those bound off on previous row. This is achieved by making a loop on the thumb and slipping it onto the needle. Continue knitting to the end of the row.

3 To avoid loose stitches and untidy corners, work into the back of the cast on stitches on the following row. Alternatively, cast on one stitch less than required, and make one stitch on the next row by working twice into the stitch immediately before the buttonhole.

Reinforced buttonhole

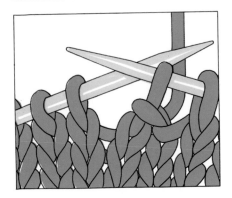
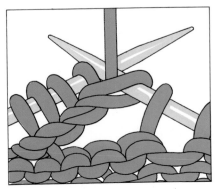
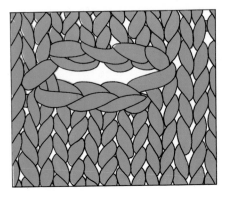

1 The reinforced horizontal buttonhole is made on one row. Knit along the row to the buttonhole position. Bring the yarn to the front of the work, slip one, take yarn to back of work, bind off without knitting by slipping the next stitch, and passing the first slipped stitch over it. Repeat this until the required number of stitches has been bound off. Slip the last stitch back onto the left-hand needle and turn the work around – do not work to the end of the row.

2 Take the yarn to the back of the work. Cast on stitches onto left-hand needle to replace those bound off, plus one extra but, before placing the last stitch onto left needle, bring yarn to the front of the work. Turn.

3 Slip the first stitch from left-hand needle to the right-hand needle and pass the extra cast on stitch over it and off needle. Continue knitting to the end of row.

BUTTON BANDS

When buttons are the fasteners on knitted garments they are usually placed on a band. This can be picked up from the main section and knitted on, or made completely separately and sewn onto the garment. If the band is knitted separately, make sure that it is the correct length. If it is too short the front fastening will not sit well. If too long, it will sag at the bottom hemline.

The band is knitted in seed, rib or garter stitch and must be of a firm fabric made to lie flat. Ribbed bands are most common.

The steps that follow show a picked up band being worked in a single ribbing.

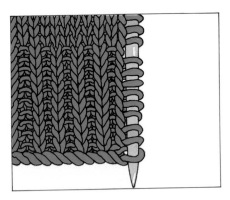
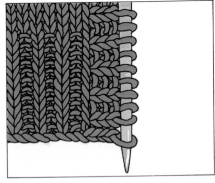

1 Allocate more stitches to be picked up over ribbed sections than on the stockinette stitch section. Work into the cast-on row at the hem edge taking the first stitch from the cast-on row to give an even edge.

2 Work in rib, but knit an extra knit stitch on right side rows at hem edge. This gives a neat bolder and stronger finish. When one stitch is knitted at the edge, the band tends to curl and give an uneven line. When the band is the correct depth, bind off loosely in rib.

SINGLE CROCHET EDGING

Single crochet edging is a perfect edging for fine knitted garments. It is often used along edges which would otherwise tend to curl, such as the selvage edge of stockinette stitch scarves or of small placket openings.

Buttonholes can be worked into a single crochet edging by skipping a stitch or two at the position of the buttonhole and working two or three plain chain stitches. Chain stitches are made by wrapping the yarn around the hook and drawing a loop through the loop on the hook.

When working a single crochet edging on the knitted fabric, use a hook that passes easily through the knit stitches to ensure a neat finish to the work.

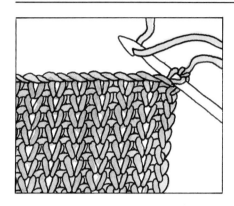

1 *Insert hook into the knitted edge that is to be covered. Wrap the yarn around the hook.*

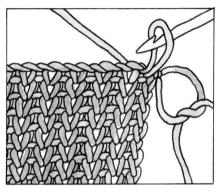

2 *Draw yarn through and knot the loose end of the crochet yarn to the knitting yarn to secure. Ends should be darned in at the back of the work later.*

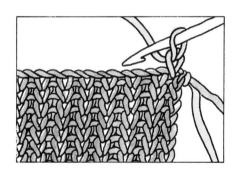

3 *Holding the knitting in the left hand, wrap the yarn around the hook and draw a loop through the loop on the hook.*

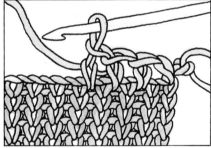

4 *Insert hook again into the knitted edge a short distance from where the yarn was joined to the knitting. Draw a loop through the knitting. Wrap the yarn around the hook and draw a loop through the two loops on hook. Repeat all along the knitted edge. If a second row is required, turn the work, chain one and then work one single crochet in each single crochet until you reach the end of the row.*

Special Techniques

EMBROIDERY ON KNITTING

Almost any embroidery stitch can be used on a knitted fabric, and even the most simple stitches can be used to produce a decorative effect. Stockinette stitch makes a good background but embroidery combines equally well with patterned stitches.

Always use a blunt-ended tapestry needle when embroidering onto a knitted fabric so the knitted stitches do not split.

Be careful not to distort the knitted fabric as the embroidery is worked. Take particular care not to stretch the knitting as you sew or pucker the work by pulling the stitches too tightly.

Satin stitch

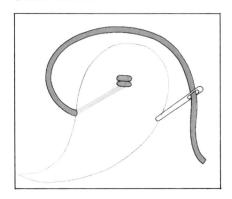

1 Secure the yarn with a few tiny stitches. Bring the needle through to the front halfway along one side of the design.

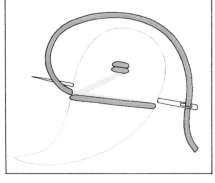

2 Make each stitch by inserting the needle on one side of the design and bringing it up through the fabric on the other side.

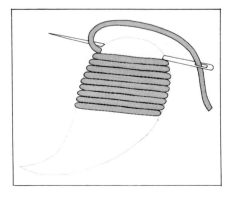

3 Continue in this way to the top of the design, keeping all the stitches parallel with the first one and close together.

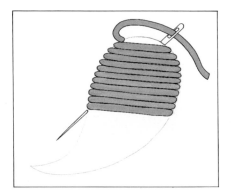

4 Bring the needle up again at the center of the shape and complete the second half of the design in the same way.

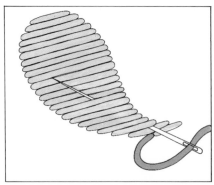

5 When the design is complete, fasten off the yarn on the wrong side under the satin stitching.

162

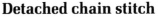

Chain stitch

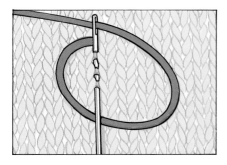

1 Using a blunt-ended needle and contrasting colored yarn, secure the yarn at the back of the work. Bring the needle to the top of the fabric and insert it through to the back. Now bring the needle out to front of work a few stitches from top, but do not pull it through.

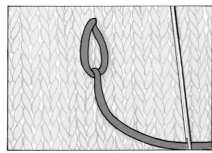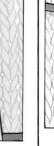

2 Form the yarn into a loop behind the needle, holding it down with your fingers. Draw the yarn through to form one chain stitch.

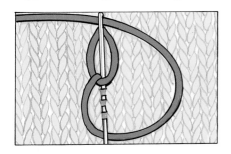

3 Now insert the needle through the bottom of the same stitch. This is now the top of the second stitch. Work as in steps 1 and 2, with a fairly loose tension.

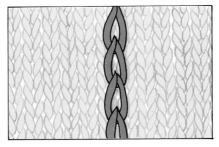

4 Repeat steps 1-3 until the chain is the required length. Keep all stitches the same length and pull the loop through evenly.

Blanket stitch

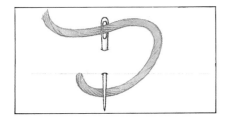

1 With the thread emerging from the back of the fabric, insert the needle into the fabric with the point emerging within the loop made by the thread.

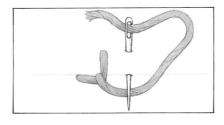

2 Pull the needle and thread through until the stitch lies flat. Continue in the same way with the stitches fairly widely spaced.

Detached chain stitch

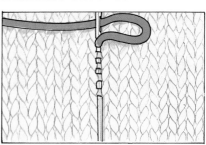

1 Secure the colored yarn onto the back of the work. Bring the needle to the top of the fabric. Now insert needle through to the back. Bring the needle through to the front a few stitches away.

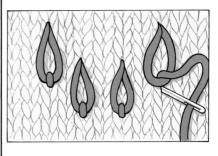

2 With the needle on the right side of the work, wrap the yarn around the needle and draw the yarn through. One chain stitch has been made. Catch the loop down with a small running stitch. This completes one detached chain stitch. Repeat steps 1 and 2.

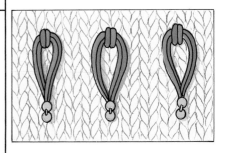

3 Simple chain stitches can be transformed by using an unusual thread such as cord, fine bouclé or a fluffy yarn. One or two small beads in a toning or contrasting color can be sewn to each stitch to add emphasis.

163

Duplicate stitch

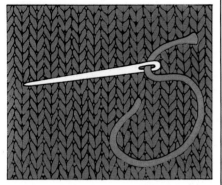

1 Thread a large blunt-ended needle and secure the yarn at the back of the work. Bring the needle to the front of the work at the bottom of the stitch.

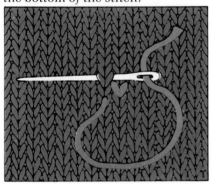

2 Insert the needle at the top of the same stitch. Pull yarn through, take the needle to the base of the first stitch. One stitch has been covered.

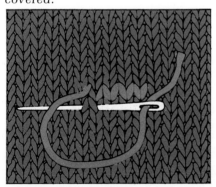

3 Working from right to left, bring the needle to the base of the next stitch, and work in exactly the same way as the first stitch.

Buttonhole stitch

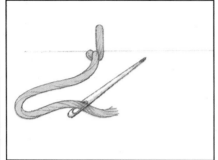

1 The first stitch should be made in the same way as the blanket stitch.

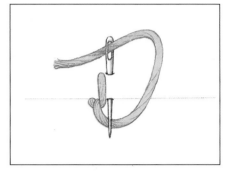

2 Insert the needle very close to the first stitch so that the finished stitches will butt up to each other.

Herringbone stitch

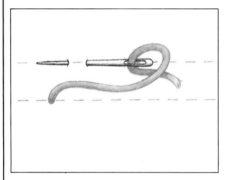

1 Bring the needle out on the lower working line and on the upper working line take a small stitch from right to left.

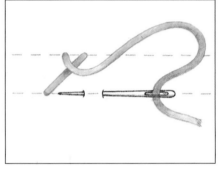

2 Take the thread over the worked stitch and make a small stitch from right to left on the lower working line.

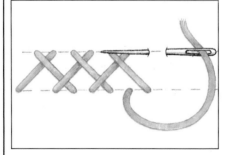

3 Continue in this way, working the stitches alternately on the upper and lower lines.

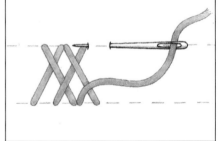

4 A firmer herringbone stitch is produced by working the stitches closer together. This is especially good for applying appliqué pieces.

Fern stitch

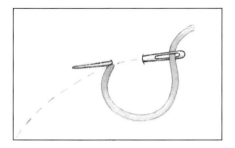

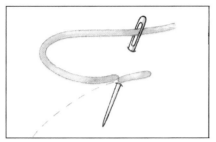

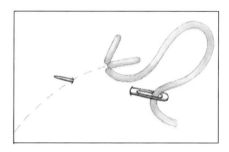

1 *Take a straight stitch along the line of working, bringing the point of the needle out in the place where the thread first emerged thus making a back stitch.*

2 *Take a similar stitch to one side of the working line, bringing the needle out in the same place as described in step 1.*

3 *Take a third straight stitch to the other side, and this time bring the needle out further along the stitching line ready to make the next fern stitch.*

BUTTONS

Handknit buttons add a personal touch to a knitted garment. They are also very practical when a bought button of matching color cannot be obtained.

A handknit button consists of a core and a knitted cover. The core can be a bought button mould, a bead or a buttonhole stitch wheel (shown here).

Circular in shape, the knitted cover should be firmly knitted, so that the stitches do not separate when stretched over the mould, allowing the base to show through. For this reason a much smaller needle size than normal is used.

Once complete the cover is stretched over the button core. The actual method of working the cover is the same, whether it is stockinette stitch, a small textured pattern or a Fair Isle type of pattern.

Button core

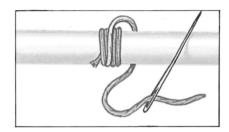

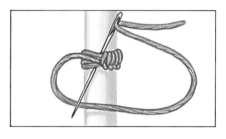

1 *Wind the yarn around a rod, which is slightly smaller in diameter than the required buttons. Leave a long end of yarn and thread onto a needle.*

2 *Work around the coil of yarn in a buttonhole stitch until a complete round has been covered.*

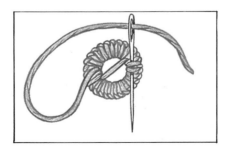

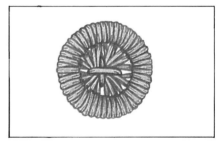

3 *Remove the coil from the rod and using the same needle and yarn, pick up a couple of stitches from the opposite side of the ring, then a couple of stitches to one side of the starting point. Pull the yarn through.*

4 *Continue in this way, working around the ring, until all the center has been filled. Work in cross stitch or a few running stitches at the center to secure the diagonal threads.*

Special Techniques

Button cover

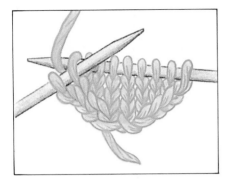

1 *Cast on a few stitches and work one row knit. Continue to work in the chosen pattern, increasing one stitch at each end of the row, until the increase edge measures exactly the same as the cast-on edge.*

2 *Work a few rows without increasing, until the straight edge measures the same as the cast-on edge.*

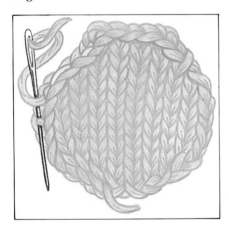

3 *Decrease one stitch at each end of every row until the same number of stitches remains as for the cast-on edge. Bind off. Work a row of running stitches around the edge.*

4 *Place the core or mould on top of the knitting and pull up the running stitches tightly, thus covering the mould. Fasten off securely.*

ABBREVIATIONS

alt	alternate
approx	approximately
beg	begin(ning)
cont	contin(e)(ing)
dec	decreas(e)(ing)
foll	follow(s)(ing)
"	inches
inc	increas(e)(ing)
K	knit
MC	main color
M1	make one
oz	ounce(s)
P	purl
pat(s)	pattern(s)
psso	pass slip stitch(es) over
rem	remain(s)(ing)
rep	repeat(ing)
rib	ribbing
RS	right side
sl	slip
sl st	slip stitch
st(s)	stitch(es)
St st	stockinette stitch
tbl	through back of loop(s)
tog	together
WS	wrong side
wyib	with yarn in back of work
wyif	with yarn in front of work
ybk	yarn to back of work
yd	yard(s)
yft	yarn to front of work
yo	yarn over (needle)
*	repeat directions following * as many times as indicated
( )	repeat directions between parenthesis as many times as indicated

INDEX